Portman's America
& Other Speculations

Portman's America

& Other Speculations

Edited by
Mohsen Mostafavi

Harvard University
Graduate School of Design

Lars Müller Publishers

Portman's America

Mohsen Mostafavi

By now I have visited and stayed at a lot of buildings by John Portman. And still, the awe of his architecture doesn't fade away. Many of these buildings are hotels, sharing common programs and approaches to their design, but nevertheless they manage to convey a particular spatial strategy that makes each one of them distinct—different from the rest.

In designing these buildings, it seems John Portman was not afraid to try new ideas and then, once he had settled on a concept, to create variations on the theme that would supply the architectural singularity of their appearance. He has designed many such buildings, which like himself possess a strong character. Often it is the repetitive and scalar nature of an element that enables the architecture to produce a different affect. And this, together with the formal and volumetric articulation of the building's interior, is all that is needed to create a dramatic experience for the user. The "use" of the buildings is of vital concern to John Portman, just as the user's experience is in turn a critical function of his architecture. This deep understanding of the relationship between the two, between user and space, lies at the root of his entrepreneurial success.

You enter one of his hotels in Atlanta, the Marriott Marquis or the Hyatt Regency, and look up. The giant shaft in the center of the building—the atrium—makes visible what was always hidden inside high-rise buildings. The entirety of the hotel is laid bare in front of you, as if Portman had decided to reach out and physically remove, hollow out, the core of the building the way a fishmonger cleans the inside of a fish.

Historically, the only surface that could be privy to the view of each floor was the opaque, unseen casing of an elevator as it shuttled up and down the building. But with these hotels, it is as if Portman vastly expanded the elevator shaft, and made the elevators in transparent glass, in order to exploit to the full the perceptual experience of traveling up and down the height of the building. This turning of an inside into an outside—where what was hidden was now revealed—produced its own sense of spectacle.

Look up and around from the lobby and you will see the whole life of the hotel unfold before your eyes. There are people looking down from the open hallways of the different floors between which the elevators move, transporting travelers of all shapes and sizes to their rooms—a mechanical ballet in slow motion. This inside-out architecture is perceived not just as a visual spectacle, but as a visceral condition. You are in the gut of the building, undergoing a sensorial, "endoscopic" experience. All is exposed to view.

The interiors of Portman's hotels from the 1970s on parallel the experience of the 19th-century railway terminals that produced such a compelling sense of the public interior. These rail stations were places where travelers, whether arriving or departing, could eat and drink and mingle in much the same way as they would in a traditional town square. The Japanese architect Fumihiko Maki, during his early Metabolist years, also pursued similar ideas connected to the notion of an urban room—an interior setting for the human interactions that take place within the city.

John Portman's evolution of the atrium, however, is a vertical as well as a horizontal concept, and the degree of privacy increases as soon as you leave the lower, more public (or rather semipublic) spaces of his buildings. The lobby, whether on the ground or on one of the higher floors of the building, is invariably the stage on which things happen and from which things are viewed. Equally, the upper-level corridors surrounding a hotel's atrium become balconies from which the action on the stage is observed. Such relations can be considered both as participatory theater and as surveillance—watching and being watched.

In Portman's hotels it is the fleeting spectacle of the simultaneous unfolding of events that captures the eye—a kind of multiscreen experience that does not require us to focus on a single event for too long. The effect is that of a panorama which draws the eye to a detail here and then there. No wonder Andreas Gursky found the interior of the Hyatt Regency, before its renovation, such a precise and fitting subject for his 1996 photograph, *Atlanta*. The single interior could stand as the representation for the whole city—its exteriority.

Looking at Gursky's photograph, the eye is captured at once by the power and drama of the repetitive elements of the whole—the balconies, the planters, the color of the carpets—and by the small variations in the form and modulation of the building. The position of the camera establishes a horizon, akin to a landscape. What is below the line reveals more and more of the horizontal surfaces of the hotel, such as its hallways, while the areas above the horizon line become more linear and facade-like. The camera is the stage, the actor, looking at the theater waiting to be filled by the audience.

1996, the year of Gursky's visit, also coincided with the city's hosting of the Olympics. A year earlier, and partly in anticipation of this event, Ramón Prat and the photographer Jordi Bernadó produced a visual volume, *Atlanta*, with an accompanying text by Rem Koolhaas, which describes the city as he found it: "Sometimes it is important to find out what the city is, instead of what it was, or what it should be." Koolhaas's journey to Atlanta was based on "an intuition that the real city at the end of the 20th century could be found there." His text about the city and about the work of John Portman is full of admonition as well as admiration: "Atlanta's is a convulsive architecture that will eventually acquire beauty." This eventual beauty, he believed, would grow in part from the topography and the climate, with vegetation, the landscape between the city's multiple nodes, performing the dual role of cover and glue—a form of stealth liminality that also gives coherence to endless sprawl.

In the absence of a creative and financially viable alternative for the redevelopment of the streets of downtown Atlanta, the Peachtree Center, begun in the early 1960s, provided a self-contained district set apart from its surroundings. This fundamentally interior world had to recalibrate the relationship between the public and the private domains of its functions and, in turn, the lives of its users.

If Koolhaas's reading of Atlanta tried to confine itself to "what the city is," then its focus on the description of the everyday parallels the concreteness with which Walter Benjamin's *The Arcades Project* (*Das Passagen-Werk*) looked at the 19th- and early 20th-century arcades of Paris. These interior public spaces, which were literally carved out of the fabric of the city to house shops, offices, workshops, and hotels, are in some sense also the precursors of projects like the Peachtree Center—not just in terms of their potential formal connections, but in their emphasis on what Susan Buck-Morss has referred to as Benjamin's "dialectics of seeing," which relies on the "interpretive power of images that make conceptual points concretely."

Following in the earlier tradition of photographs of Atlanta by Gursky and others, *Portman's America* uses the photographs of Iwan Baan to document John Portman's architecture. Baan was commissioned to travel to the sites of projects across the country,

Andreas Gursky, *Atlanta*, 1996

Jordi Bernadó, *Atlanta*, 1995

from Atlanta to San Francisco, from Detroit to New York City. The resulting photographs, rather than being formal or idealized images of buildings, capture the view as if in a state of distraction; Portman's architecture, and by extension Portman's America, is presented as it is today, for all to see.

Often images of fragments, the collection of photographs begins with Portman's two homes. Entelechy, in Aristotelian metaphysics, is the complete actualization of potential intentions and visions. The images of Entelechy I, Portman's Atlanta house, capture some of these desires in their descriptions of the building's relationship to the outside, an aspect of crucial importance to John Portman. But it is the treatment of the in-between spaces—those between the inside and the outside, those involving the use of water—which best expresses the specific character of the building. In one photograph, the inner facade of the building is defined by rows of two-story columns; outside this, a brick wall made up of semi-circular elements filled with plants rises only one story below the house's projecting roof. The combination creates a shaded outdoor space, a calm retreat from the interior as well as the garden of the house.

The second house, Entelechy II, on the shores of the Atlantic Ocean in Sea Island, continues the theme of interplay between inside and outside. Rather than being carried out just on the ground floor, the sense of the explorations here is very much three-dimensional. At Sea Island, Portman has created an environment that occupies three distinct yet interrelated zones—the interior, which brings in the outside, including nature; the covered and semicovered outdoor areas, which combine architecture and landscape in equal measure; and the outdoor proper, which is still engaged with traces of architectural elements.

The naming of these two houses, as well as the manner of their realization, provides one of most cogent demonstrations of John Portman's interest in the Aristotelian concept of hylomorphism. Architecture, as a physical object, the embodiment of being, is conceived here as the combination of matter and form. It is in this sense, too, that Portman insists that the role of the user of his buildings cannot be separated from their conceptualization. Each project is the consequence of the coming together of the body, as matter, and form.

This emphasis on the importance of the experiential helps to explain John Portman's desire to integrate within his buildings not only his art work, including his sculptures, but also furniture of his own design. It could also be said that the strong desire to move from potential to actualization to some extent provides the justification for Portman's role as a developer. He learned early on the benefits of being able to play a major role in the implementation of projects, above and beyond the conventions of contemporary practice.

Apart from the use of photography to capture the everyday "facts" of the buildings, this book includes other speculations that help unfold John Portman's contribution to architecture. My colleague Scott Cohen's decision to base his spring 2015 option studio on the exploration of what he has called *Portmanian Architecture* has provided an opportunity not only to assess Portman's work but also to consider its potential as a catalyst prompting a group of Harvard graduate students to conceive and construe another architecture. In many respects the impetus for this publication came out of the respect and admiration many of us have developed for John during our interactions with him at the GSD over the past few years.

Complementing the studio work are two critical essays by Jennifer Bonner and K. Michael Hays and Alexander S. Porter, the latter linking two generations as it acts as a hinge between the earlier projects of John Portman and Scott Cohen's own work. Finally, there is the conversation between John, Mack, Merrill, and Mickey, a group of friends just talking together in a manner and tone that affords the reader at least a glimpse of the mind and the personality of John Portman, an icon with an inclusive and fearless vision of America and its architecture. When John gave me one of his books some years ago, he wrote "for Mohsen" and then underscored, all in capitals "THE LIFE IS GOOD."

And I believe him.

How can you get yourself involved if you don't know yourself? I don't know.
I just know it's necessary.
I think we're all unique.
And I came with my baggage, so it's unique baggage.
There'll never be another me.

JP

The following conversation between John Portman, Mack Scogin, Merrill Elam, and Mickey Steinberg took place at Portman's home on Sea Island, located on the southern coast of Georgia, and at the new Portman-designed Hotel Indigo in Atlanta.

Mack Scogin How long have you been coming down here?

John Portman We came down here in the '50s when the kids were small. We liked Sea Island. We would rent a house, and Jan would stay down here most of the summer. I would come in on a Thursday night and go back to Atlanta on a Sunday night. The kids had a ball, because they could run free all over the island. We didn't have to worry about them. It's still that way. But now they put up a gate.

MS The last time we were down here you just drove onto the island. I think the hotel was redone since we've been here.

There's a spa over there. It's probably one of the fanciest spas you ever saw. They added a hundred rooms... sixty-five, I think.

MS I think you have to wear a black tie for dinner.

No, but you have to have a coat for dinner. I couldn't get in with these dungarees on.

MS You have creases in your dungarees. They'll let you in. My mother used to starch and iron my Levi's. Everybody would laugh at me.

I'm glad you told me that. Now I know why all those people have been laughing at me.

By the way, Merrill, it's John. Mr. Portman's my dad.

Mickey Steinberg Guess how long it took him to design this house.

All my life. You're walking through my life when you walk through here. I decided to let a few people in, like Picasso, to share with me. It's not a house, it's a place.

Take the site, take the island—if you go back to when man started using the beach for recreation, you started to see an umbrella stuck in the sand, blankets underneath, people reading a book or something. That's the house. The umbrella is the roof. The house rests underneath taking in nature. The encapsulating of the house with nature conceals it in a way such that it doesn't impinge on the rest of the place.

I talk about making space with the exploded column. Here, when I built this house, I was going to have a wall go down on either side to protect it from the tourists. I decided I'd split the wall, move it out, and make a space—a special series of small sculpture gardens on the site. There's a certain time of year that the sun comes right through here and this whole thing lights up. It's unbelievable.

That's my rickshaw chair. It's all one line. See how that water separates? See how I planned the lighting, the way the grid hits the wall?

The house is about 12,000 square feet. If you take the whole space, thirty-something thousand square feet. It's just like another world.

> **MS** My reaction to it is that it's a world house. It's a house for the world. It's like the most modest house you could build for the world. I came away thinking this is your masterwork.

I think it probably is.

I wanted to compose music for this house. Yo-Yo Ma went to Italy and played his music in cathedrals. He was bringing those spaces alive. Sound is important. Movement means a lot. If I develop a plan, I can walk in it and visualize it in three dimensions, play with the volumes and orchestrate the movements. I can do that. Subconsciously, I do that. I can say, "Well, this ought to happen there."

MS And you're looking at a drawing, right?

MST He's sitting around a table with a couple of designers. They're working on a little bitty sketch about this big. He draws a little line, and he says, "Look how monumental that is."

In my mind, I'm in the thing I'm working on. I'm in there. I'm walking up, turning the corner. Architecture flows like music from space to space with some consideration. Frank Lloyd Wright was good at dropping the ceiling as a segue to something else. It's compression and release, and compression and release. It's an articulation, how you handle terminations and connections. Scale, knowing scale. If I have a room that's 16 feet by 16 feet, what happens if the ceiling needs to go a little higher? You have to be able to crank that thing up in your mind. Where does it stop? Right there. Move it a little bit, it's wrong. You can see that in reality.

MS How do you get that ability?

I don't know, it just showed up.

Back in the Depression, in the early '30s, we certainly didn't have anything. As a kid, in the backyard, I would take medicine bottles and visualize them as cars. I would build hills and valleys and the roads. I would take this bottle up over the hill and down. I had a feeling for that. Whatever the hell that means. I've been lucky because, you know, you're just lucky. You're born in such a way, you can do certain things, and you can't do certain other things. I'd give anything if I could play the piano. I can't play. I don't have the slightest idea how I got anything built. I just play with the tools I've got.

I love the world of ideas. Will Durant's book, *The Story of Philosophy*, is an order of trips through Western philosophy, from Socrates to Santayana. One of the first things Socrates says is, "Know thyself." How can you get yourself involved if you don't know yourself? I don't know. I just know it's necessary. I think we're all unique. And I came with my baggage, so it's unique baggage. There'll never be another me.

There'll never be another you. Architecture is not only a question of sight, it's a question of feel. Without even thinking, you say, "Well, that feels good. That feels great."

I've never taken a risk. It's not a risk in my mind, because I've thought it through this way, that way, this way, that way. I'm not interested in the latest fads. I am interested in the development of everything that relates to what we as humans do. I'm surrounded by books. The truth of the way we live and think, and everything else, is in transition. Now there are new things out there that are causing that. I'm interested in those things. If I want to use banana, but I've never tasted banana, I've got to get in there and understand banana first. It's all common sense.

MS You're making more like uncommon sense than common sense.

Well, as somebody once said, "Common sense ain't common."

MS Your mother?

When I opened my own office, in a little 300 square foot room, my mother told me to go and borrow $100 and pay it back, and then borrow $150 and pay it back—to build a history for yourself.

My mother didn't graduate from high school. She finished as a freshman. I mean, hell...my mother was just brilliant. She was one of the most brilliant human beings I've ever seen. She was something else, I'll tell you. She painted too. Grandma Moses kind of painting, but she painted. She grew up here in Atlanta. She worked, during the Depression. She was so pragmatic.

She helped me develop a lot of the ways I'd think and do. She said, "If you get knocked down or something bad happens to you, you got to look at it like a wreck on the freeway. You get up, it's happened, nothing you can do about it. You look forward, and you look forward enthusiastically and positively. And you don't dwell on it. You don't replay that scene over and over again. That's done. That's gone. Now, let's go." I remember that because I used that in the '90s.

You got to believe in yourself. You got to have confidence, faith. You got to have conviction. You got to have discipline. And you got to learn how to focus, and to prioritize.

Merrill Elam Was your mom happy?

Oh yeah, she was 89. She was a chain smoker.

ME What were you doing in the Naval Academy during World War II? Was that interesting for you?

I was 19. I graduated from high school on a Friday night, and I was drafted the next morning. Every year they have 200 fleet appointments to the Naval Academy. The rest are congressional appointees. I didn't know any congressional people. I wasn't interested anyway. I wanted to be a fighter pilot. You had to be in the Navy for a minimum of eight months before you could be transferred into the flight programs to become a pilot. They sent me to aviation ordinance school in Millington, Tennessee. I learned how to synchronize shooting bullets through a propeller and, blindfolded, take apart .50-caliber machine guns and put them back together again. I was putting in my eight months.

I double-bunked with this kid who wanted to go to the Naval Academy. I was on the lower bunk, he was on the top bunk. He had this *Annapolis Today* book. Every year they would come and have a bake off. This kid talked me into going down there. I told him I wasn't interested. He was nervous, and he wanted somebody to keep him calm. I agreed to go down there with him. We go in and they gave us this test. Anyway, I'm outside sitting on a log waiting for him to come out. He's probably the next to last guy to come out. He had been sweating bullets. When they announced the results, they said, "Hear ye! Hear ye! The Annapolis detail results are posted on the bulletin board." Boom! He came flying out of that top bunk. Zoom! He was running down there. I got up to go see how he made out. I go down there and my name's up there, but not his. Isn't that ironic? I didn't want it. But after I got it, I decided I'd take it.

They were giving everybody these crew cuts. All the guys hated it. The barbers loved it. I found out I could cut hair. I set up a little barber shop in the barracks. I had them lined up and I was cutting their hair. I cut just enough so that they'd pass.

In Annapolis, they put me on the boxing team and I had three days to get prepared for a bout.

ME Did you know anything about boxing?

I had worked out in the gym and somebody saw me hitting the bag or something. I just know that they threw me in there. We had a little guy coach us, Spike Webb. He was about this tall. This little fellow. He was the coach. He said, "Son, I'll tell you one thing: you fight a boxer and you box a fighter." I said "Okay. Who am I fighting?" He said, "They got you marked down over here on the list. Do you want to come see it?" It was Piasoky, the champion of the South Atlantic fleet. He said, "But son, he's a boxer. He's just going to dance. He's going to win on points. You don't have to worry about him. You go in there and you do a Marciano." The bell rang, I went out there. I didn't lay a glove on the guy. He beat the hell out of me. When I came out of the ring, I do remember that Spike Web came over. He said, "Kid, I told you to hit the man. You hit everything including the corner post, and you hadn't touched the guy."

Long story short, I ended up 189th on the list. Just barely got in. I was there for over a year. VJ-Day was August 14, 1945.

> **ME** You left the Naval Academy, and that's when you came back to Atlanta and went to Georgia Tech, right?

Right. I was on the GI Bill. I had to make a little money there, too. I set up a little tutoring thing.

When I came back to Tech, they wouldn't give me all the credits that I had at the naval academy. I already had the first year's course. It was a breeze. I was charging these GI's who were fighting to get a position. We made a little money there.

> **MS** You went to Georgia Tech. The obvious question is, why would you go into architecture?

I did architecture in high school. I was harboring that all the way through. Up until the third grade, I did murals for classes. They'd have fairs, school fairs, and I'd do all the decorations. Even at Georgia Tech, I did all the decorations for the Beaux-Arts Ball. In high school I was into athletics— basketball, football, all that stuff. I was hyper with energy.

I'd see these guys in the drafting class sitting over drawings, and I'd say, "Hell, I'll never be able to sit still that long." I put it off until I couldn't graduate unless I took that course. I go in there and it was like duck to water. I was in the ninth grade, and the teacher came over and said, "Son, have you ever thought about architecture?" I said, "Hell, I don't even know how to spell architecture."

When I was at Tech, they would take my projects and put them in the morgue [the archive]. Right before I left Tech, I went into the morgue, took them all out, and destroyed them.

> **MS** Why did you do that?

When I was at Tech they had a big Hugh Stubbins retrospective. I said, "God, I don't want them doing that to me."

P.M. Heffernan [the director of the architecture school] used to come around at midnight. He'd sit down, and if the guys were not there, he'd leave a little note. "I see that you are not here. I suppose you don't have enough interest in architecture."

I don't know if I told you I'm an old man, 92 years old.

> **MS** You're not 92, that's a number.

It's a number, but don't let me repeat myself. I'm sensitive about that, because I never liked to hear old guys repeat themselves.

My dad died in '89. He was a chain smoker.

My dad worked for the GSA. He was in the real estate section here in Atlanta. They were in charge of all the government buildings. When I had this little tiny office, my dad called me and said, "Listen, I just got word that they're moving out. They're going to build their own building. Why don't you go down and talk to Mr. Henderson. Maybe you can get a potential job out of this."

So, I did. Before I went in there, I went and cased the building. If I was going to meet Henderson, I wanted to have an idea for him. I came to the conclusion that you can take their building, which was once a parking garage, and turn it into an exhibition hall. Atlanta didn't have any exhibition halls. I went in and I said, "You know, Mr. Henderson, I heard that you're moving out. I think you could put a merchandise mart in here." I went on and told him why. He says, "Son, I'm too old to go into anything like that. I don't know anything about that business. I'm too old to learn. I'll turn it back into a parking garage."

I thanked him and I started to the door. I had the door open, ready to go out, and he called me back in. "Listen," he says, "I've got an idea. Why don't you go form a corporation and I'll lease you the space at 50 cents a square foot. I'll give you a five-year lease with a five-year option. I'll help you with the tenant improvements. I really don't want to go back to a parking garage." I laughed and I said, "Well, thank you. That's an interesting thought." I left his office, and as I got down to the street I started thinking maybe there was something to that.

Anyway, a fellow midshipman from the Naval Academy was in Atlanta and he was managing the old Peachtree Hotel. They had been using the hotel for trade shows a lot, so I went and explained everything to him. He said, "We have a childrenswear show going on right now. Let's see what old Charlie Schulman has to say." Schulman, he was all excited about it. He says, "My god, that would be wonderful."

That was the beginning of it. I formed the corporation and negotiated the deal. Part of the deal was that I only pay for the space I use. If I wasn't able to lease it out, then I didn't pay for it. I filled the building within a year. 250,000 square feet. We were getting recognized in the industry and we needed more space. I was the agent with my partners. I'd go to the shows and go from booth to booth talking to potential tenants.

MS But you were an architect?

I was an architect. Right.

Griff Edwards, he was my partner. He was a prince. I was so tired of doing houses…I thought, fast, you got to move faster. I called Griff up and I put down specifications on what that partner had to look like. He had to be at least 15 years older, since I was losing jobs because I was too young. He had a little gray hair, was 15 years older than me. I wanted somebody who loved what he did as much as I loved what I did. I hated specifications. I wasn't going to administrate a damn thing, because I didn't want to have to wonder if anybody stayed 15 minutes beyond their lunch hour.

Anyway, he loved all that stuff. When it came time to do the development, I went to him and told him, "Here's the situation, Griff. I want you to come in with me. I don't cost you any money, because I don't have any money. It's just an idea. We'll work on it, we'll find it."

That's how that thing started. That is a *Gone With the Wind* story. Coming from nothing, I mean, zero.

MST Today the AmericasMart is about seven and a half million square feet.

It's appraised at 1.3 billion [dollars] now. We're number one. The reason we're number one is because Atlanta's airport is the busiest airport in the world. We have all the connections.

MST I've often said to John, "You know, the most important conversation you ever had was that one with your dad."

MS It's amazing. If my dad would tell me to do something like that, I wouldn't do it. I would just say, "Well, thanks a lot, dad. That's really good. I'll keep that in mind."

You don't understand that at the time I owed him 150 dollars.

I opened my own office in 1953. After I'd done two or three houses, I decided I'll never make a living on this. On one house, I figured I made 31 cents an hour. I came to the conclusion, all you really got is time. What are you going to do with your time?

I made a decision, I wanted to do significant things. I didn't want to do just anything; I wanted to do significant things. It was that kind of simple observation. So I started developing the Wilby-Kincey building, which I designed when I was a student. It was behind the Fox Theater. The theater needed a parking lot at night and Bob Wilby needed it in the daytime for the office workers. So I put it on stilts.

Mr. Wilby took a liking to me. I realized, before anybody can build anything, you have to have a piece of land. John O. Chiles was the dean of the real estate people here, and he was a friend of Bob Wilby. I got Bob to call up John O. and get him to see me. John O. went on to be my agent. We put together all this land. I just had ideas, I didn't have any money. We got 99-year ground leases, and I was calculating I'd get enough money out of the parking fees to pay for the ground lease. I end up getting control of the land for free, in a sense, until I was ready to use it. And that was part of the masterplan process.

Once I had the Mart, I had enough money to build a house. A lot of architects don't want to build their own house, because you can't blame it on the client. Even Saarinen didn't build his own house. He took an old house and converted it.

Architecture is not about things, it's about people and life. When I tried to understand how the two are related, I asked myself, how did architecture start? What's its essence? It started with the column. The column, first, is a tree trunk, and then another tree trunk, and then a span between.

I wanted something that had scale and that could stand the test of time. Taking the column, I decided that what I'd really like to have is a living pavilion—a pavilion created by columns. I have the column totally integrated; it's not only the structure, but also a spatial thing that would give me the scale I want. Eight feet was the dimension I came up with that I could use as galleries, study rooms for the kids, closets, powder rooms, or connections from one space to another as you circulate through them. I maintain the idea of the pavilion and I blow out the top so I get daylight that spews through.

A scale with the major and minor spaces and no halls. What are the kind of spaces that fall into this kind of category? I call it exploded column. I took eight feet, then put eight feet between the exploded column in eight pieces—north, south, east, west. The diagonals come and go depending on function. I can have it completely enclosed with just one opening. You got to know why you're doing something and what you're trying to accomplish.

I'm interested in people. I sit in spaces all over the world and do nothing but people-watch. I watch them react to certain things, see their innate responses, and look for the truth to jump out and tell me something.

Search for truth, and that's it. You do that, you're not vulnerable to fads. You're making, like God would do it, from the ground up. It's evolving, and that's what life's all about. Life is, from the beginning to the end, a question of something evolving, a movement.

Think holistically. I call it expose/impose. I want to expose everything about the circumstance that exists. And somehow grab onto it and make it do whatever it has to do.

People think the house was built in the last few years. They don't realize it's 50 years old. But see, that's the classical nature of the thing. It's done in a way that it stands the test of time.

The column is the structure of architecture. I had played with that idea of exploding the column, and its functionality. The column can do more than just structure. Break it up into eight leaves, you create diagonals. The four leaves that are opposite each other are the structure, and in between you can come and go depending on the function. You put them in, take them out. Four of the leaves have been taken out.

The other thing—and this is something that Kahn talked about—are the major and minor spaces. That was on my mind. I had just visited with Kahn at Joe Amisano's house. I got an opportunity to corner Kahn, and I had just been to his Yale building, where he did this tetrahedron. They put partitions all the way to the ceiling, so I asked, why the span?

I explode the column to the correct dimension that would allow me to put the minor functions in, eliminate the hallways, and make the house a pavilion. Everything in it would close and open to make a pavilion. I had stairwells, art galleries, kids' study rooms, closets, outer rooms, and books all over. It ended up being very classical, like some Greek temple.

That's another thing—scale. I could have held that house up with two columns.

MS I remember going to visit your first house as a student. I remember thinking it wasn't wild, just unique. It could have only come from you.

That's right.

> **MS** Who were the people in Atlanta that were your champions?

J. Paul Austin, chairman of Coca-Cola. Ben Massell, who was the biggest developer at the time. John O. Chiles, who was the number one real estate guy. Mills Lane, the banker. Jim Robinson, another banker. I don't get to know bankers, they get to know me.

> **MS** Did you know Martin Luther King?

I did not. Now, interestingly enough, I integrated the first two restaurants here in 1961. The top of the Mart and the bottom of the Mart.

> **MST** When the Hyatt Regency first opened, it was integrated.

They opened in May of 1967. Mick's right, it went integrated from day one. But we'd already set the stage from '61.

> **MST** Another thing he did was open the first kosher kitchen in the city, inside the Westin Peachtree Plaza.

We formed the Action Forum. It's probably the most important organization during that period. It really was a powerful group. The group was made up of 10 members from the white community and 10 from the black community. You had to be the head man of your company to be on Action Forum. Because they wanted all the decision makers around the table. They didn't want a bunch of vice presidents taking messages back. If you couldn't come, then you couldn't send anybody. You were just absent. That's the way it operated.

The first thing we took on was MARTA [Metropolitan Atlanta Rapid Transit Authority]. We got MARTA passed. I'll never forget, I was in the Amigo Hotel in Brussels when the vote came in. I got a call from Atlanta. MARTA had passed by four hundred and something votes. And it had been defeated three or four times before. I was doing cartwheels around the room. We had gone all out, both the black and the white members, through this Action Forum. It was the first thing we sponsored. It was a very effective group. Marshall Hahn of Georgia-Pacific, Coke, Delta Airlines, all the banks. The chairmen of all the banks were there. We had a black chairman and a white chairman. On the white side, some of us who were not bankers decided that the only chairman we could have had to be a chairman of one of the banks. Because if he's there as chairman, all the others are going to show up. It worked like a charm.

MS It was apolitical.

Absolutely. No politician could be on it. You had to own a company. You had to have something at risk. Never had the problem that everybody else did. Never had the riots.

Andy Young is one of my closest friends.

The Regency was such a success that within 90 days the Pritzkers [the hotel's owner] wanted to add a 200-room addition.

When we opened, we had 10,000 people trying to get in. It came about by recognizing how people use central city hotels and how traveling creates a lot of anxiety. I wanted to bring them into a place that was almost a resort in nature. You ask yourself, which I did back then, what is a central city hotel like? It has a lobby, and it's usually a meager lobby, and there's maybe a little gift shop over in the corner. You come in, you register, you go into this box of an elevator, you go up, you come out into this little space and get into a narrow double-loaded corridor, and it's a window and an outside wall. That's it. I wanted to open it up. I said, "Well, hell, let's pull the elevators out of the wall." I pull the elevators out of the wall. One thing leads to another. It's going to be like a movable sculpture. A space within a space.

We were the reason for the Pritzker Prize.

After the Regency, I started orchestrating buildings as if it was one. I was doing a 70-story tower and I only had a 50-foot piece of land. I brought the core down and I cantilevered the 200 rooms out over the ballroom. This little round addition in that position made all the solid rectilinear buildings make more sense.

On a bigger scale, I came up next to the old Davidson building and I had to get 1,200 rooms in there. I had 200 feet, so I did a big round tower. Now this little round tower over here and the big round tower over here begin to tie together.

So now I come to the Atlanta. I've got this cubic form, and these slab forms, and these round towers. I'm going to put all these forms together into this one, and that's what I did. You get the parabola at the base, and it comes back to a slab.

I was getting bigger and bigger and bigger, but I didn't want to have a big firm. I didn't want 500 people. Good God! It's hard enough for me to keep up with what I had to keep up with. If you're a detail freak like I am, you want to get down and touch everything and make sure that everything's just the way you want it. It's not possible, but that's the way it is.

I came to the conclusion, whatever I do, I'm going to get me a structural guy, and I'm going to get a mechanical guy, and I'm going to get an electrical guy, and I'm going to get a landscape guy, and I'm going to get a graphics guy, and have an interiors department.

I did all that. But I had just one. I wasn't going to build departments around these guys. This structures guy, anything related to structures went through him. I had one guy to see. Same way with landscaping, or design lighting, whatever. Because it's all the same. It's the same sheet music. You have to control that sheet music...

> **MS** You were one of the first Western architects to practice in China. How did that happen?

When Deng Xiaoping came to Atlanta, I was asked to put him up. So I put him up on the 70th floor of the [Westin] Peachtree Plaza hotel. He was blown away.

We went to China in 1979. I was invited by Governor Busbee, because I gave Deng Xiaoping a room on top of the Plaza. Deng Xiaoping wanted to open China to the West. That's what Shanghai Centre was all about. It's now landmarked. Look what's happened to China. I told the secretary over there, "My God, you went from the stage coach to the all electric car all in one sweep." How did they do it? They bought the best technology, they had the cheapest labor, they controlled everything—so they took capitalism and socialism and merged it.

> **MS** John, back then were you looking at other architects' work? Once you were out of school, once you started your own practice, once you didn't have to look at other architects' work, were you aware of what was going on in the broader profession? Did you think about that? Did it effect the way that you were thinking?

I'll just say I was aware of it. I'm a voracious reader. I know what is going on in the profession, but I've got my own agenda. My own agenda is one that's in search of a new truth. Immanuel Kant said all reality is man-made. Take your mind and make your own reality. And you perceive your reality, as we all do, through the five senses. You can orchestrate these, and let them play with each other so they make sense. I have to feel the space. If you can't feel the space, you're just riding the circus. I play with scale. Emerson says the answer lies in nature, is nature. So I try to pull nature into the buildings. Fountains and trees and flowers and all that kind of stuff, because we are nature, we are indigenous to nature.

In San Francisco we did this floating veil over the cocktail lounge. On top of it, I put a row of speakers. I put these little speakers in different places, and then I recorded these birds singing. They come in a flock, and then they land. One will answer from over there, and another will answer from over there. I remember when it first opened, I'm sitting with this reporter from the *San Francisco Chronicle*, and here come the bird chirps…

The answer lies in nature, the evolution of forms, all forms in nature. Do it as God would do it—that's nature. I'm always trying to find a uniqueness in a set of circumstances that's not different just to be different, but indigenously unique. And to take that uniqueness and spin out from that uniqueness.

Take this place, for instance. When I mirror that wall next door, it doubles the space and it doubles the trees. With one row of trees, you get an alley of trees and make a horizontal atrium. I'm looking for that uniqueness, a genuine truth that lurks below.

I think if you're interested in design, you can design anything. Design is design. As long as you've got the facts, you can work with it, whether it's got wheels or not, it doesn't matter.

I talk about doing things holistically. I designed furniture, lighting fixtures. I even designed cocktail uniforms for the gals serving drinks at Midnight Sun. Somebody had to design them. Don't laugh at this, it's the truth.

I did this thing—a mini skirt thing? Anyway it came down. I had to come up with a collar.

MS One of my and Merrill's favorite projects of yours is the Dana Fine Arts Building at Agnes Scott College in Atlanta. How did this unusual building type for you come about?

Griff got this commission. They wanted us to house painting galleries, sculpture galleries, and a little theater. The students all wanted a modern building, but the faculty, they wanted a Gothic building. I now had to satisfy both sides of the table, or at least I felt I did.

Actually, it's a very modern building. It's a building within a building. I used the brick as a buttress, you know, the weight. I wanted to walk through something, not go up to the door and just go in. So I created this space in front of it. And then I exploded the thing. I layered these painting galleries. I finally got past both the students and the board, who couldn't believe that I did it. I really didn't sacrifice a hell of a lot in getting there.

Dana had given them the money, and he happened to be cripple. He was from the Detroit area. He had something to do with auto transmissions, made all this money. The board got a call that he was coming into Hartsfield on a plane. He didn't have time to come out to the school. He would like the architect to bring the drawings to the airport. I get a call from the president. The president says, "Well, we'll all go with you." I must have had six of them from the board. We go out there, and they put us in this little meeting room. They wheeled him in there and he sits there. I take the drawings over, just a line draft. He stares, and he says, "Why did you grade it like this?" I said, "Mr. Dana, I graded it that way because that's the way it should be graded." He pushed his wheelchair out, rolled up the drawings. I thought everybody in there was going to fall out on the floor. He threw the drawings at me, and he said,

"Young man, you go build it, and you and I will have a party."

We don't say it's what Mr. Portman's trying to do. We find a way. Everything really comes back to common sense. I always wanted to do an all glass stair. Damn it, I did it.

     MS Is that logical?

No.

     MS I didn't think so. I just wanted to make sure.

I don't know what the hell I'm going to do next, I really don't. But I know how I'm going to approach it; I know the way I am, the way I feel, the way I see. These passing phases in architecture don't mean anything to me. I'm interested in the latest materials or the latest techniques. Due to advances in technology, we are living in a time which is probably the most condensed time of change the world's ever known.

I've got to tell you, it's been fun. It is still fun.

     MS You've done all of this, and you've raised an amazing family. How many kids do you have?

Six. Five boys and one girl. They all have engaging personalities, unlike their dad. Dad's too damn busy to worry about personality. I'll tell you something, they're all characters, believe me.

     MS Well, John, come on, what do you expect? What the hell did you expect?

Strong personality—it is a good thing.

What do you think of the Four Seasons being thrown out? The Four Seasons. That's unbelievable.

I talk about making space with the exploded column. Here, when I built this house, I was going to have a wall go down on either side to protect it from the tourists. I decided I'd split the wall, move it out, and make a space—a special series of small sculpture gardens on the site.

JP

Entelechy I
Atlanta, GA, 1964

On 30 wooded acres in the Buckhead neighborhood of Atlanta, a gridded forest of 24 cypress-clad columns define both the structural system and spatial life of Entelechy I, the first of two houses designed by Portman for his wife and six children. From the Greek word ἐντελέχεια, the name knowingly intertwines aspiration and declaration, indicating both "the final form of a potential concept" and "a vital principle." Indeed, here, the essential qualities that would define Portman's wide-ranging   are on display: the evenly spaced columns alternately enclose and explode, hiding private studies or revealing winding staircases, anchoring the walls of private bedrooms or framing the flowing space of a music room for public entertaining. The dramatic main entrance brings in guests by bridge to a second-level foyer, hovering over an indoor stream that floats the formal dining area in its center. From the balconies, Entelechy I overlooks downtown Atlanta, where Portman would continue to exercise his imagination through the formation of a new skyline.

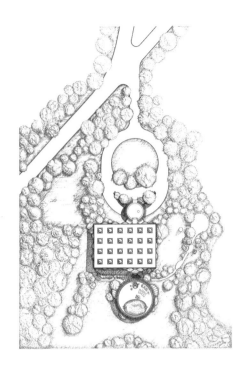

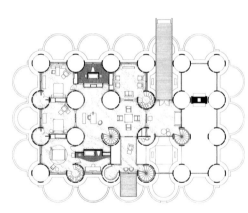

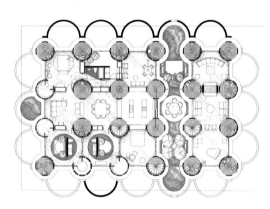

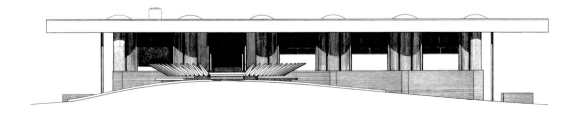

Entelechy II
Sea Island, GA, 1986

The second home of the Portman family stretches out on the shores of the Atlantic Ocean in Sea Island, Georgia. Eighteen exploding columns echo the structural DNA of its suburban predecessor, Entelechy I, but reconstitute themselves in the sculptural exuberance of a complex of four living pavilions. Dressed all in white concrete and crawling vines, the pavilions spring from reflecting pools and levitate over terraces, completing every view with planes of water or sky. Ramps and bridges take guests over, through, and beyond the edges of the enclosed interiors, providing a variety of paths

through the studio and museum, which showcase the Portman family's art collection as well as Portman's own large-scale artworks. The four pavilions—a glass living and dining pavilion, a two-story entry wing, a suspended master suite, and a freestanding guest house—luxuriate under the cover of a deep rectangular sunshade. The grille is supported by an array of columns and two exaggerated outriggers, one extending inland over the grand entry stair and the other toward the outdoor pool and the ocean beyond.

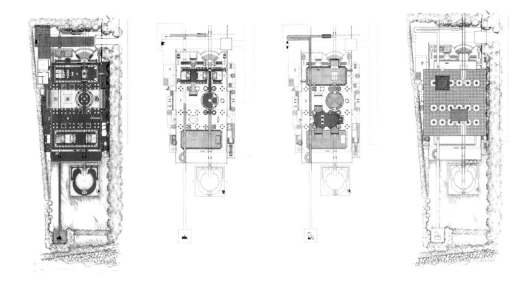

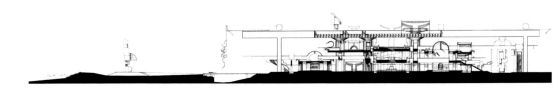

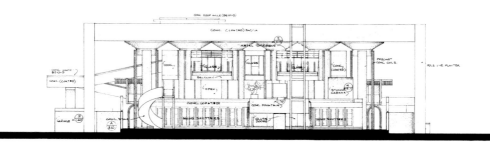

A lot of architects don't want to build their own house, because you can't blame it on the client. Even Saarinen didn't build his own house. He took an old house and converted it.

JP

When I opened my own office, in a little 300 square foot room, my mother told me to go and borrow $100 and pay it back, and then borrow $150 and pay it back—to build a history for yourself.

JP

John Portman in his Atlanta office, 2016

AmericasMart (Building 1, 2, and 3)
Atlanta, GA, 1961–2008

The AmericasMart is comprised of a trio of buildings: Building 1, formerly Atlanta Merchandise Mart (1961, addition 1968/1985); Building 2, formerly Atlanta Gift Mart (1992, addition 2008), and Building 3, formerly Atlanta Apparel Mart (1979, addition 1988). The Atlanta Merchandise Mart occupies the corner of Peachtree and Harris Street (renamed John Portman Boulevard at Historic Harris Street in 2011) like a downtown pavilion, a perfectly square bundle eight bays wide and eight bays deep, eschewing both curtain walls and rows of punched windows for a more reticent facade. White structural columns and long strips of windows flow uninterrupted from rooftop to sidewalk, vertically segmenting ridged panels of precast concrete. The facade itself stops short of the ground level by one floor, creating a sidewalk arcade that allowed the street in to meet the lobby. At the time of construction, the Atlanta Merchandise Mart was already the largest building by floor area in Atlanta, but it would soon metastasize into a three-building complex known as the AmericasMart, connected to the original building and to the rest of the Peachtree Center developments by a series of glass skybridges.

The Atlanta Apparel Mart occupies a full city block directly north of the Atlanta Gift Mart, which was constructed on top of another Portman project: the 1968 Continental Trailways Bus Station and parking garage. The Apparel Mart's square plan is anchored at four corners by sculptural exterior stair towers. In 1988, Portman added seven stories to the original nine-story Apparel Mart. The stark solid and void striations of the circular towers make a graphic statement against the building's windowless concrete facades. Inside, the floors are arranged around a fan-shaped central atrium, with balconies oriented toward a small stage and the main elevator bank at the southeast corner.

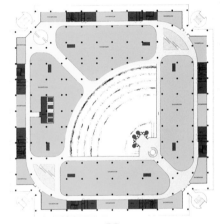

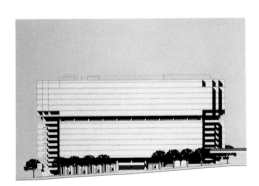

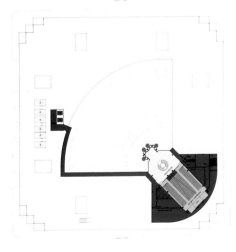

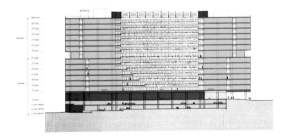

Peachtree Center
Atlanta, GA, 1961 – ongoing

The 14-block development comprises 18.9 million square feet of office, hospitality, trade mart, and retail buildings. Bisected by a boulevard bearing Portman's name, the Peachtree Center development is home to an array of iconic Portman works, including the AmericasMart, Atlanta Marriott Marquis, Westin Peachtree Plaza, and Hyatt Regency Atlanta.

Peachtree Center developed over time:
– Atlanta Merchandise Mart 1961, addition 1968, 1985
– 230 Peachtree Building 1965, renovated into Hotel Indigo 2016
– Hyatt Regency Atlanta 1967, Ivy Tower addition 1971, Peachtree Street tower addition 1982
– North Tower and Midnight Sun Restaurant 1968 (originally Gas Light Tower)
– South Tower 1970
– International Tower and shopping gallery 1974 (originally Cain Tower)
– Harris Tower and Midnight Sun Dinner Theater addition to shopping gallery 1976
– Westin Peachtree Plaza 1976
– Atlanta Apparel Mart 1979, addition 1988
– Atlanta Marriott Marquis 1985
– Marquis 1 office tower 1985
– Marquis 2 office tower 1988
– Inforum Technology Center 1989
– Peachtree Center Athletic Club 1989
– SunTrust Plaza 1992
– Atlanta Gift Mart 1992, addition 2008
– SunTrust Plaza Garden Offices 2000

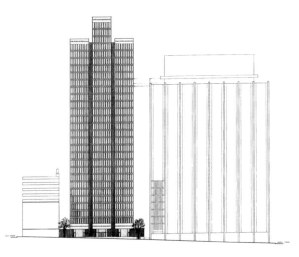

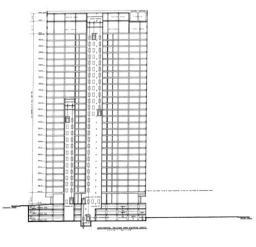

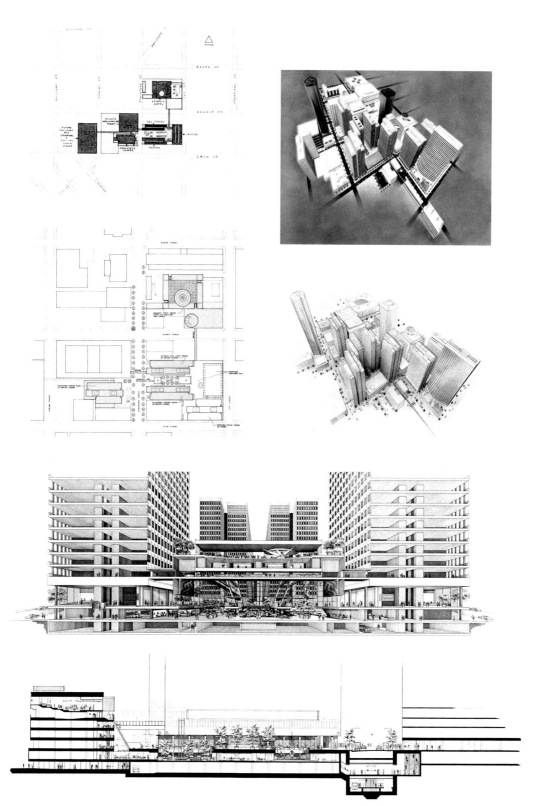

109

Hyatt Regency Atlanta

Atlanta, GA, 1967

The Hyatt Regency Atlanta was the first of Portman's atrium hotels. Refusing to replicate the packed double-loaded corridors of conventional hotels, Portman exploded and evacuated the hotel interior, creating a public, garden-like lobby that continues vertically for 22 stories. A giant circular skylight illuminates the space from above, creating an uncanny simulation of an open-air environment. The first iteration of the iconic glass elevator cabs that would zip through all of Portman's hotel atria made its debut here. All the hotel units were pushed to the building's perimeter and corridors were left open to overlook the central atrium. Staggered along the edge, a series of dark metal guardrails and rectangular trellises were designed with the look and feel of outdoor balconies, hanging vines and all.

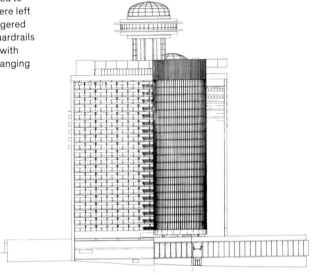

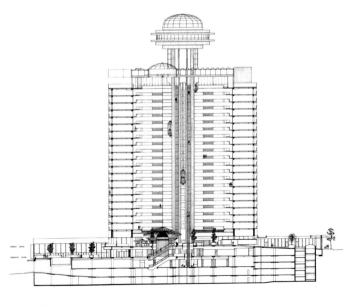

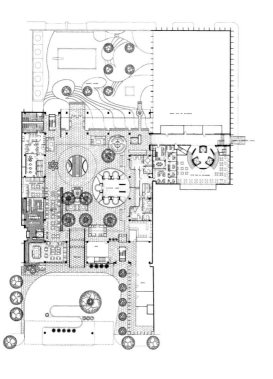

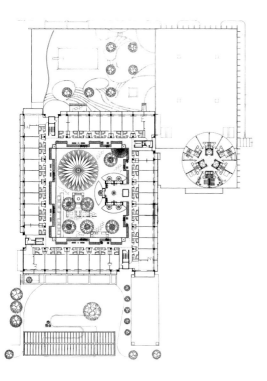

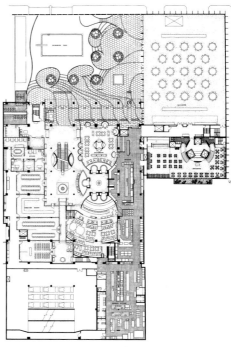

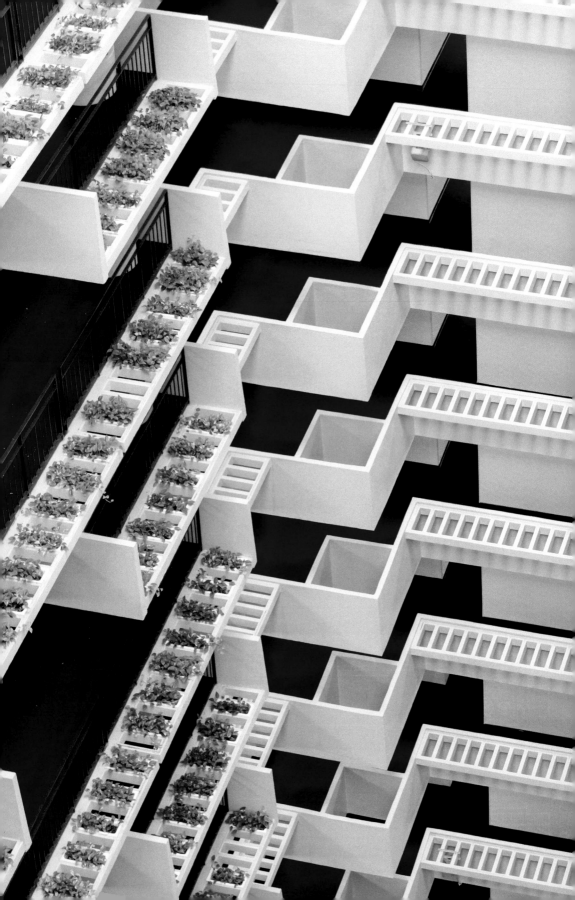

Westin Peachtree Plaza
Atlanta, GA, 1976

The Westin Peachtree Plaza fills a long, narrow site on the southern edge of the Peachtree Center. With the Hyatt Regency Atlanta, Portman's first atrium hotel, just a block and a half away, the Westin presented an opportunity to create an entirely different kind of urban proposition. Rather than enclosing its magnificence inside a hidden atrium lobby, the hotel asserts itself boldly in the Atlanta skyline: a 73-story, mirror-clad cylindrical tower in the crowd of rectangular mid-rises constituting Peachtree Center. While today the lobby strikes a more conventional pose, decorated in carpet and lounge seating, its original incarnation was similarly fantastic: the five-tiered main atrium featured an indoor lagoon, hosting a wonderland of fountains, cocktail lounge islands, hanging sculptures, and floating trees. The sloping site allowed the podium to accommodate a lobby on the same level as the pedestrian street entrance to the east, while slipping the vehicular drop off underneath the lobby to the west, two levels below.

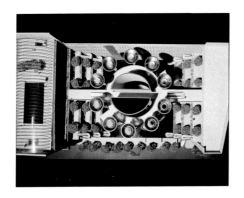

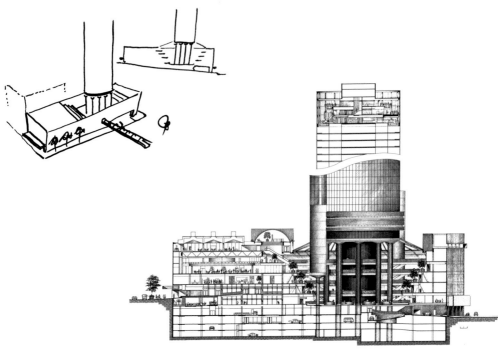

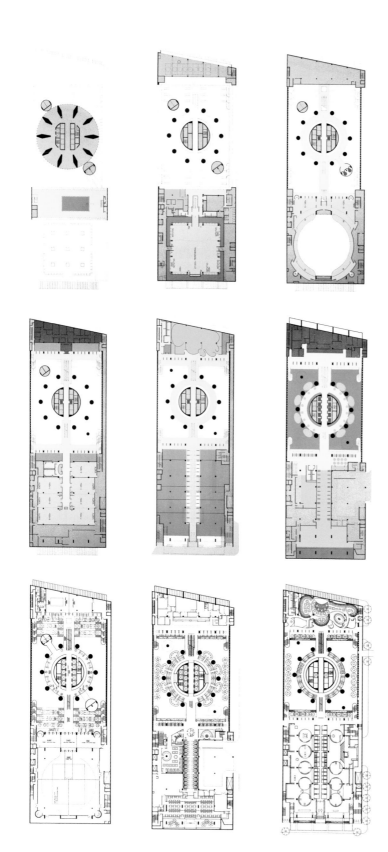
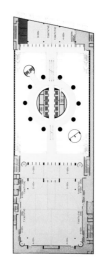

141

Atlanta Marriott Marquis
Atlanta, GA, 1985

The Atlanta Marriott Marquis occupies the majority of an entire city block, occupying the ground level between and around the twin Marquis office towers on Peachtree Center Avenue. A covered porte cochere anchors all three buildings at street level, setting the 52-story tower of hotel rooms back from the street. The setback gives the otherwise slender tower room to swell at its base, an evocative ripple in the facade suggesting that it has yielded to an unexpected pressurization of the 515-foot-tall atrium within. Indeed, looking up into the seemingly endless succession of riblike bands gives the impression of peering inside a living organism. The lobby floor anchors the public life of the hotel in a plaza decorated with trees and symmetrical curving walkways. At the center of the lobby plan, a cylindrical core hosts 13 glass elevator cabs and connects to select floors with a series of dynamic footbridges.

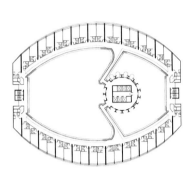

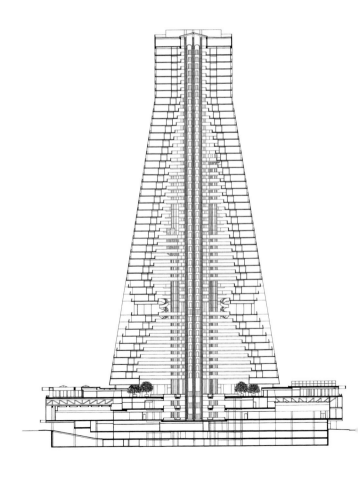

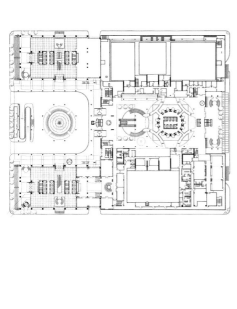
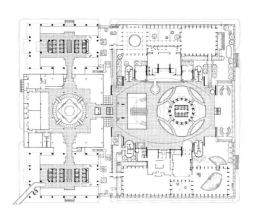

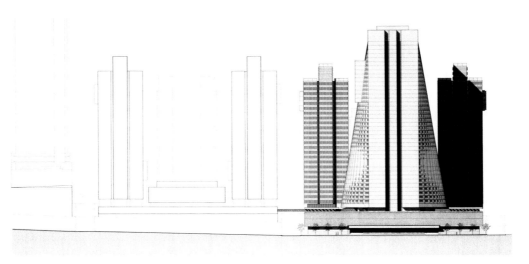

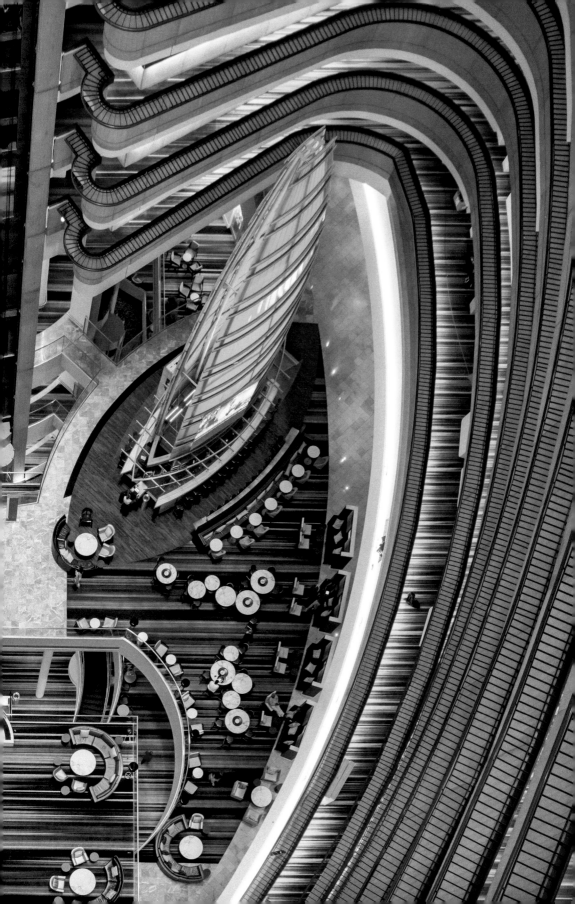

Inforum Technology Center
Atlanta, GA, 1989

The Inforum Technology Center, now known
as the American Cancer Society Center, was
originally intended to be an integral
component of the AmericasMart trade mart
buildings. Its full-block square plan is cut
along a central north-south axis, with circular
terraces scalloping the edge of its rectangular atrium. The atrium lobby is lined
with massive exploded columns, five-story
versions of the sculptural columns found
at Entelechy II, and capped by a gabled
skylight. The building's four glass facades
reflect the skyline of downtown Atlanta,
virtually reducing each face into a grid of
fine curtain wall mullions, the antithesis
of the solid concrete mass of the Apparel
Mart next door.

Atlanta Decorative Arts Center
Atlanta, GA, 1961 (expansion 1971, 1977, 1982, and 1986)

The Atlanta Decorative Arts Center was
one of Portman's first business ventures, complementing the establishment of the trade
marts downtown by housing a leading regional
resource for interior design professionals.
The five-story, 550,000 square foot building
in the Buckhead neighborhood of Atlanta
is a deep display of showrooms arranged along
the perimeter of the building and accessed
by interior balconies which overlook a rectangular atrium, brightened by skylights
overhead and a palette of white walls and rails.
The center simulates the rhythms and
atmosphere of an outdoor, urban pedestrian
mall, with floors connecting across the central
atrium via a series of vine-laden bridges.

Emory University Student Center
Atlanta, GA, 1986

In 1984, Emory University in Atlanta challenged Portman to triple the size of its student union building, the historic Alumni Memorial University Center, but preserve the Center's beloved classical marble facade. Portman, in turn, designed the R. Howard Dobbs University Center, an addition that amplified the facade tenfold: first, by transforming it into the defining interior backdrop of a three-story skylit atrium; then, by cladding the new addition in the white and gray marble for which the original facade was known. The atrium, now known as the Coca-Cola Commons, pins together old and new, east and west, and hosts three tiers of dining and gathering space overlooking the interior courtyard. Students stream into the center from all sides: the freshman dormitories to the north; the physical education center to the west; and the academic buildings of the quadrangle to the south. The amenities provided in the new addition—including a post office, cafeteria, and ballroom—are organized around a second atrium, which leads to the west entry terrace on Asbury Circle.

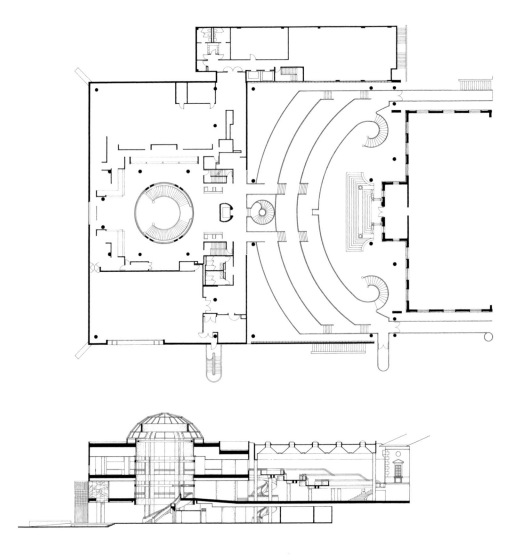

EAGLE
CONVENIENCE

Renaissance Center
Detroit, MI, 1976 (Phase I)/1988 (Phase II)

As its name suggests, the Renaissance Center was designed to revitalize the outskirts of downtown Detroit. The multiuse complex was commissioned by Henry Ford II as an investment and a public statement of commitment to Detroit, which had begun to suffer from depopulation and neglect. The first phase of the development incorporated a hotel (which would immediately become the tallest feature of the skyline), four office towers, and a multistory podium of retail and public amenities. The perfectly cylindrical central column of the hotel serves as the organizational and visual heart of the original complex; it rests atop a ring of interior columns in the six-level, tree-filled atrium below. A 13-lane highway along the northern edge of the site separates the complex from the city center, prompting Portman to orient the grand entry of the podium southward, toward the river. Twelve years later, following the opening of a Detroit People Mover station, two additional office towers were added to the complex.

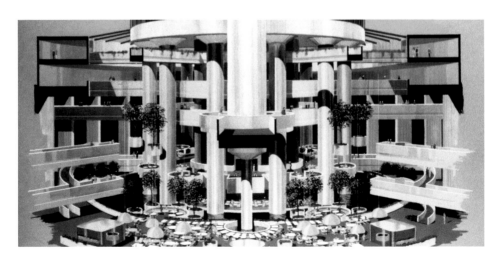

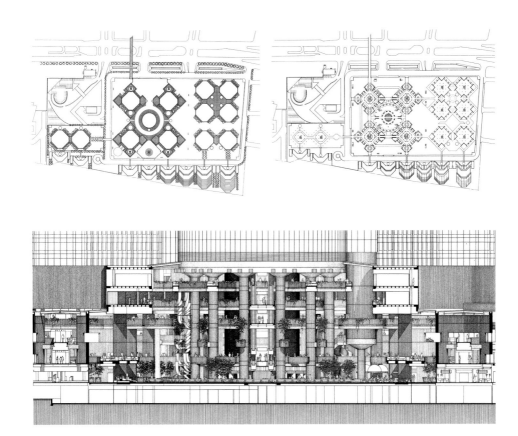

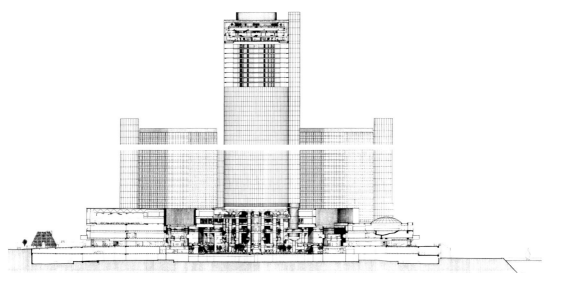

197

Architecture flows like music from space to space with some consideration. Frank Lloyd Wright was good at dropping the ceiling as a segue to something else. It's compression and release, and compression and release. It's an articulation, how you handle terminations and connections. Scale, knowing scale. If I have a room that's 16 feet by 16 feet, what happens if the ceiling needs to go a little higher?

JP

Embarcadero Center
San Francisco, CA, 1971–1982 (Embarcadero Center West expansion 1988)

The eight-block mixed-use development transformed a warehouse district into a pedestrian-friendly urban retail mall. Built in phases over a span of nearly two decades, the Embarcadero Center integrated 4.3 million square feet of new office, retail, and hotel space into the city of San Francisco while opening up a swath of open-air plazas in the dense downtown fabric. The development is centered on a primary spine of four mixed-use tower-and-podium buildings. Each tower is composed of a series of slender slabs, stacked and staggered to fill half of a city block, while each podium is camouflaged into the street as a

three-level retail building, designed to occupy the remainder of the block like an independent pavilion. All four towers are connected by a multilevel string of landscaped plazas. Here, the dynamic exuberance of Portman's hotel lobbies is translated to an exterior setting: the courtyard at the center of each block hosts a multistory outdoor sculpture, and a series of horseshoe staircases and bridges transport pedestrians through the mall. The development is completed by the Hyatt Regency San Francisco to the east and capped by a 30-story office tower, a hotel, and the renovated Old Federal Reserve Bank of San Francisco to the west.

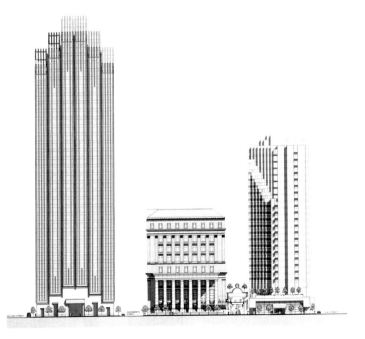

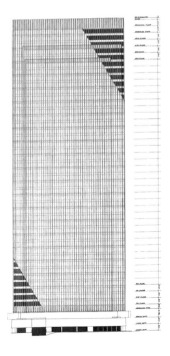

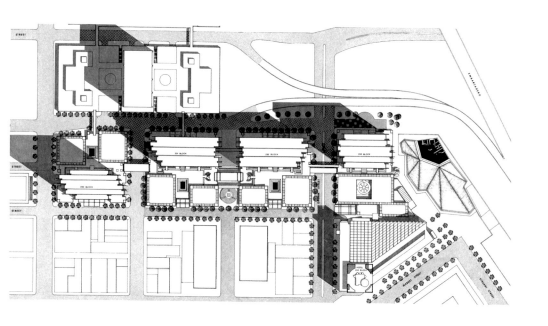

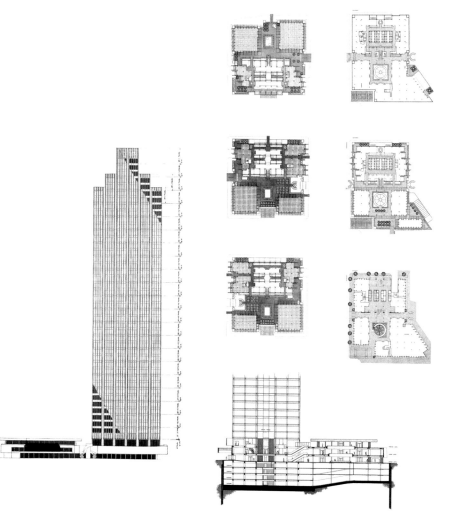

213

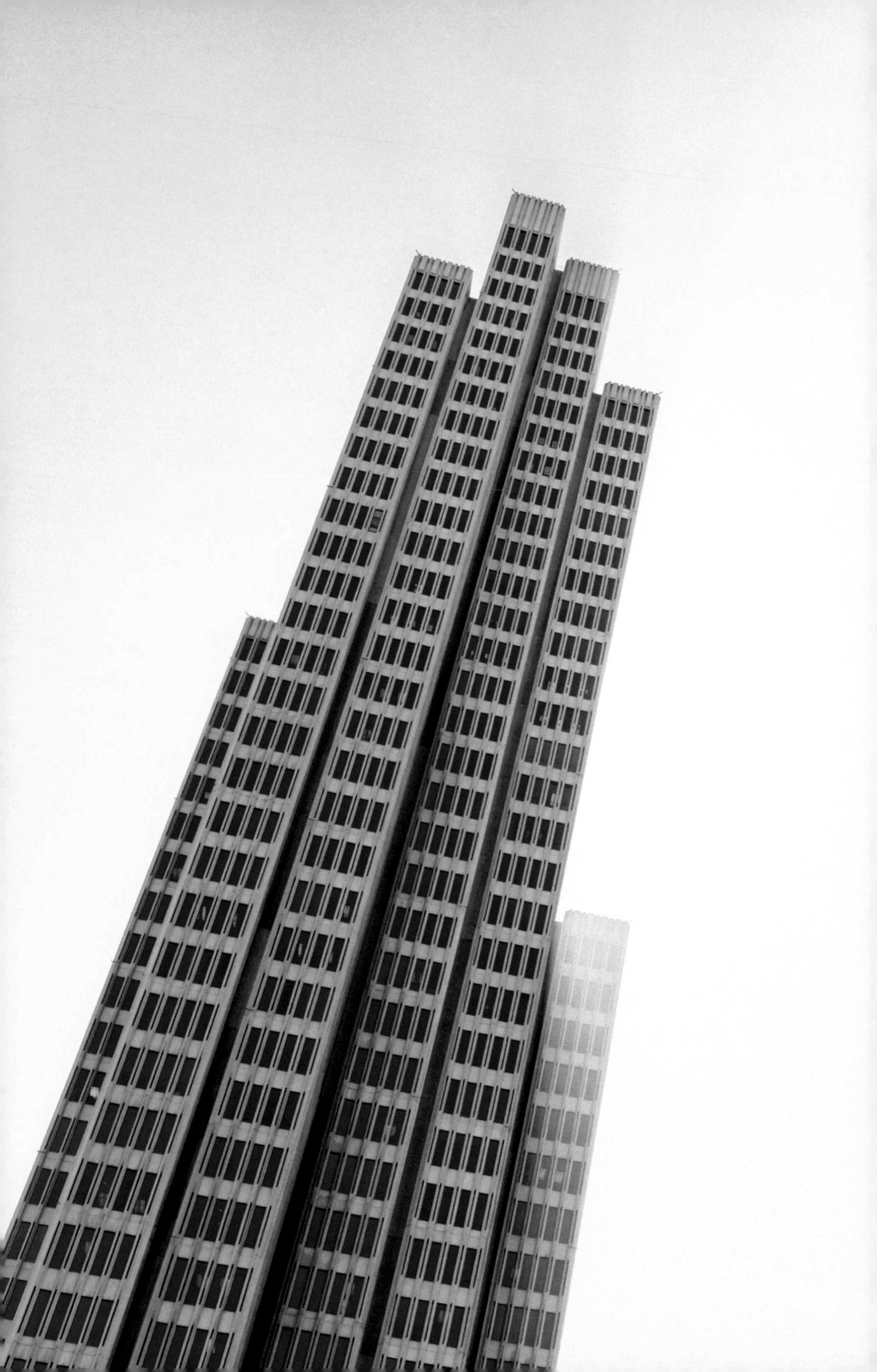

Hyatt Regency San Francisco
San Francisco, CA, 1973

The two defining grids of downtown San Francisco collide at Market Street, a three-mile-long thoroughfare stretching southward from the bay to Twin Peaks. The 30-degree shift in orientation results in a northern street front lined with wedge-shaped extrusions. But just before Market Street terminates at the Ferry Building on the water's edge, the Hyatt Regency San Francisco presents an alternative solution. Between two 20-floor wings that dutifully match the height and demeanor of their downtown neighbors, a web of terraced sunlit balconies comprises a cascading facade on the north side, gradually descending to the level of a lively plaza and the pedestrian mall of the Embarcadero Center. Inside the hotel, the two vertical wings of hotel rooms and the prismatic facets of the north face enclose a 17-story atrium. While the original revolving penthouse restaurant is now a stationary club for VIP guests, it still brings together 360-degree views of the city and the bay.

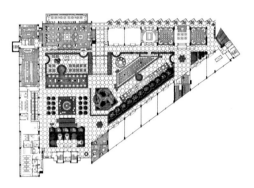

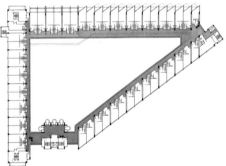

New York Marriott Marquis
New York, NY, 1985

The New York Marriott Marquis was designed as a key component of the revitalization and extension of Times Square. A theater at street level acknowledges the hotel's home in the heart of the theater district, rubbing elbows with such storied neighbors as the Richard Rodgers Theatre and the Music Box Theatre. While the building occupies an entire city block, the hotel's 1,875 rooms are divided among two slender towers and a less disciplined stack of volumes are sandwiched in between. The staggered stacking produces a set of covered outdoor terraces and massive skylights, rare luxuries for midtown high-rises. The main lobby on the eighth level hosts the fantasy of a tree-lined public plaza, which, at the time of opening, defiantly contrasted with the vehicle-dominated intersection of Seventh Avenue and Broadway. The cylindrical elevator core at the center of the 37-story atrium terminates at a rooftop restaurant and lounge, which turns the gaze of its guests out to the city.

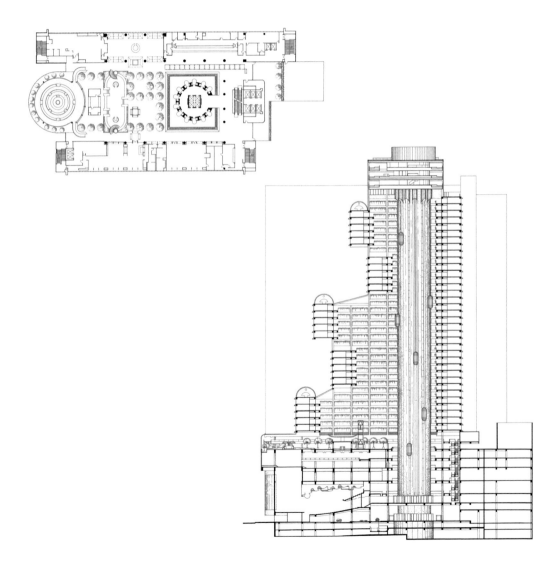

Westin Bonaventure
Los Angeles, CA, 1977

Traveling north on Highway 110 in Los Angeles, the approach to downtown is signaled by a sudden snarl of traffic, a series of swooping overpasses, and a cluster of flat-faced high-rise towers. Just behind the front line of stone and steel financial office buildings, the five cylindrical towers of the Westin Bonaventure Hotel & Suites shimmer as if made of water, mischievously reducing the reflections of its neighbors to slender, pixelated fingers. Here, as in Atlanta at the Westin Peachtree Plaza and in Detroit at the Renaissance Center, the fantastical columns so often found on the interior of Portman's buildings are scaled up to become space-makers in the city at large, and the spatial organizers of a city writ small within the podium below. The six-level podium contains the public amenities: the hotel lobby, restaurants, and four tiered floors of retail. Four exterior cores send guests shooting through the sky in scenic glass elevators from the atrium below to the hotel floors and restaurant above. Skybridges extend from the podium at various levels to connect to the surrounding buildings. Inside, cylindrical forms abut and overlap at every scale, from restaurant banquettes to elevator cabs to the wide arcs of its retail terraces.

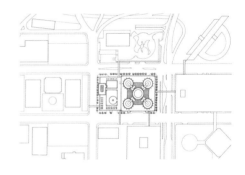

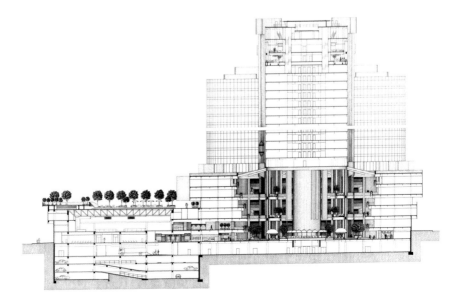

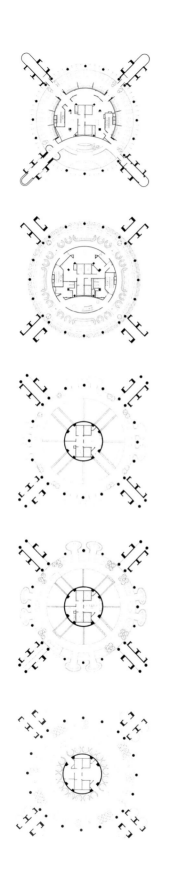
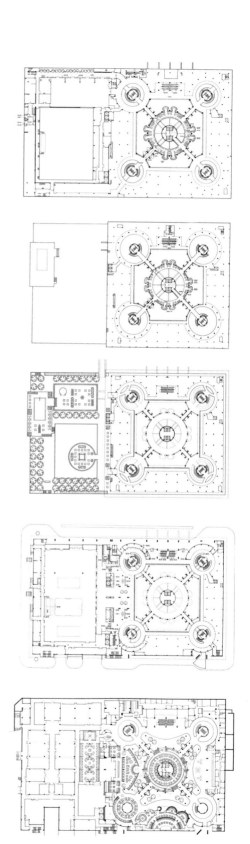

Escalator
Directory
Restrooms /

Hyatt Regency, Atlanta, 1967

Westin Bonaventure, Los Angeles, 1977

The Theatrical Paradox of the Atrium

K. Michael Hays and Alexander S. Porter

You are in a large space white with marble, inundated with light...
Tiny doors and immense openings. You are captivated, you have lost
all sense of usual scale. You are overcome by a sensory world unto
itself that tells you what it meant to tell you. What emotion! What
faith! There, that's the driving intention. The bundle of ideas is the
means that has been used.
—Le Corbusier, *Toward an Architecture*[1]

And what must have changed since Le Corbusier described the
visceral, disorienting scale of the Green Mosque in Bursa? Returning to the ancient and immutable, Le Corbusier contends that
the particular organized immensity of the mosque's interior consti-
tutes a kind of *ordonnance* affective—a set of rules (controlling
spacing, lighting, and rhythm) that relay intention and meaning,
and of which the viewer's emotion is the register. With regard to
the mosque's space, the contention advances an argument attest-
ing to the reciprocity of the interior and the exterior. For Le Corbusier, "the *outside* is always an *inside*,"[2] which is to say that an interior
results when the elements of architecture impress themselves
onto their surroundings, leaving space as their inverse cast. Lam-
pooning the figuration of the Beaux-Arts as the mere "illusion of
the plan" whose exterior shape is predetermined, Le Corbusier
sets high stakes for his claim to rediscover in ancient space the
very goal of modern architecture—an unencumbered clarity of intention to produce profound affect. "Without historical allusions,
you feel the architecture."[3]

While we might want to redeploy Le Corbusier's poetry in a first
attempt to narrate the famous Atrium by John Portman (we will
treat it as a singularity here), the challenge remains that another
capable critic should have entered Portman's Westin Bonaventure
hotel in the early 1980s to notice a rather different effect of the
experience, together with a historicity that would preclude Le Corbusier's analysis as a viable model for Portman:

This latest mutation in space—postmodern hyperspace—has finally
succeeded in transcending the capacities of the individual human
body to locate itself, to organize its immediate surroundings per-
ceptually, and cognitively to map its position in a mappable external
world. It may now be suggested that this alarming disjunction point
between the body and its built environment—which is to the initial

bewilderment of the older modernism as the velocities of space-craft to those of the automobile — can itself stand as the symbol and analogon of that even sharper dilemma, which is the incapacity of our minds, at least at present, to map the great global multinational and decentered communication network in which we find ourselves caught as individual subjects.[4]

For Fredric Jameson, who built his model of postmodern perception in part on Portman's Atrium, the obdurate exclusion of the viewing subject from the massive space nevertheless occupied represents the generally disorienting alienation of the new mode of production of global capital. On some level, this exclusion is no different from the overwhelming emotion that Le Corbusier embraced as a fundamental logic of architecture's discipline. The machines Le Corbusier employed as models for design now reappear as instruments of disorientation and dystopian detachment. But the emotion, according to Jameson, is desubjectified and "depthless." "This is not to say that the cultural products of the postmodern era are utterly devoid of feeling, but rather that such feelings — which it may be better and more accurate to call 'intensities' — are now free-floating and impersonal, and tend to be dominated by a peculiar kind of euphoria."[5]

Indeed, perhaps the same peculiar alienation-jouissance that Jameson identifies as the Bonaventure effect is responsible for the frequent use of the Atrium in dystopian popular films, including series such as *Divergent* and *The Hunger Games*.[6] If Portman's buildings appeal to the dystopian imagination for reasons similar to those Jameson articulates, it is because the exclusion of perceptible space from built form also necessitates the exclusion of the subject as individual. In these films, that exclusion justifies treating the buildings as ancient remnants or prospective ruins whose steadfast persistence as collective representations exceed the time of their mortal occupants.

We face a paradox: we can laud Portman's Atrium as a paradigm of architecture's ancient power to move us profoundly, but we do so anachronistically, as a dystopian fantasy. Or we can confirm the contemporaneity of the Atrium even as we lament how it spectacularizes our historical incapacity to find an image for the vast global net of capital in which we as individuals are caught.

The art historian Michael Fried noticed in the paintings exhibited in the Paris Salons of the 1750s a related dilemma, which amounted

Jean-Baptiste Greuze, *Un Ecolier qui étudie sa leçon*, Salon of 1757

Preston Scott Cohen, Herta and Paul Amir Building at the Tel Aviv Museum of Art, exterior, 2011

to a fundamental shift in representation.[7] The paintings, Fried argued, began to abandon their former "theatricality" in favor of a new strategy of "absorption." "A painting, it was insisted, had to attract the beholder, to stop him in front of itself, and to hold him there in a perfect trance of involvement.... It was only by negating the beholder's presence that this could be achieved: only by establishing the fiction of his absence or nonexistence could his actual placement before and enthrallment by the painting be secured."[8]

The characters in the paintings are all presented with the same *oubli de soi*—an "absorptive" state in which the depicted characters' losing themselves operates also to negate the spectator's presence as beholder of the painting while, paradoxically, securing the emotional involvement in the painting nevertheless beheld. Take, for example, the schoolboy in Jean-Baptiste Greuze's portrait, "an image of absorption," Fried calls him, whose downward gaze conveys "an impression of unseeing abstraction."[9] The painting's very ignorance of the viewer's presence works to arrest the viewer's attention.

Interpreting Diderot and his contemporaries, Fried argues that absorption is a recurrent criterion for 18th-century critics to rescue portraiture from the theatrical spectacle of the Rococo.[10] The longstanding justification for this criterion is a "fundamental preoccupation with *pictorial unity*"[11] based on disciplinary rules which are autonomous from the presentation of painting to a viewer and immune to the indictment of theatricalizing performance. Excluding the fictive spectator gives the actual spectator greater access to the discipline of painting. Just as Le Corbusier traces an understanding of space and plan to a disciplinary history of architecture through his ordonnance affective, Fried demonstrates his ontology of absorption at the very heart of painterly tradition. At stake in "the assimilation of expression to absorption"[12] is the idea that artworks engaged in an absorptive project access transcendent truths otherwise mired in the theatrical subjugation of painting to beholder.

Insofar as consistency and legibility are the hallmarks of absorptive unity, a similar notion is imbricated in the lineage of late 20th-century architects and historians who count Le Corbusier among their primogenitors. The well-traced territory on which Rudolf Wittkower, Colin Rowe, and Peter Eisenman played out their mathematics-of-the-ideal-villa project evidences internal geometrical consistency as the most valued criterion of the villa type, meaning that the object itself claims unity by the total inward absorption this consistency engenders.

In that tradition, evidence of absorptive thinking is nowhere clearer in contemporary work than the exterior carapace of Preston Scott Cohen's Herta and Paul Amir Building of the Tel Aviv Museum of Art. Oscillating between a revetment of sheared planes that meet at common vertices and a torqued, tessellated crystal, the exterior turns away from the beholder to look more deeply inward. Faced in opaque stone and devoid of fenestration, the main facade refuses to acknowledge the regard of a spectator (similar to downcast eyes of Greuze's *ecolier*) whose curiosities might otherwise be assuaged. In the case of Cohen's project, the inward turn is literal, as the disjunction between the rectangular galleries and triangular site is resolved in a clamorous atrium, which the architect calls the Lightfall.

Acting as Diderotian critics, we could view this atrium as completely absorptive, pointing to the geometric precision of surfaces, the diagrammatic disposition of apertures, and the choreographed daylight effects as evidence that the object is engrossed in a set of operative logics and disengaged from its presentation to an audience. The exterior of Cohen's project offers an architectural analog to understand the significance of Greuze's painting for Diderot, as well as an example of an atrium absorbed in its own formal machinations, in stark contrast to those we find in Portman's hotels. We can claim this contrast in Fried's terms: Cohen's atrium, with its internalized autonomous operations, is absorptive, while Portman's is theatrical. Whereas the Lightfall bypasses the question of presentation altogether, the Atrium taunts its viewers with continuous exhibition. Let us, then, test this hypothesis.

In Charles Rice's recent photograph of the Hyatt Regency in Atlanta (1967), the obsessive rhythm of balconies passes beyond the photograph's borders, without beginning or end, without foreground or background. The photograph's *studium* is the demonstration of size, of massive scale, but it is without resolution.[13] For it seems that nothing can hold the space of the Atrium, despite its immediacy, proximity, and even strange familiarity. Consequently, as viewer, I have no indication where I am standing, what the circumstances of my body are. Details and contingencies only further confound me. Each balcony has a plant, and 68 doors are visible, every one of them closed. But, on the lowest balcony, a cleaning cart has been left, marooned in the space of presentation to which

Preston Scott Cohen, Herta and Paul Amir Building
at the Tel Aviv Museum of Art, Lightfall, 2011

Marriott Marquis, Atlanta, 2009

Hyatt Regency, Atlanta, 2009

Atrium of AmericasMart Building 3, Atlanta, 1989

it does not belong, like a set-piece from a previous scene that an ill-fated stagehand neglected to remove before the curtain's ascent.

In Michael Portman's photograph of the AmericasMart Building 3 at Peachtree Center (1979/1988), an unassuming glass box surprises visitors with a theatrical, fan-shaped atrium of stepped terraces. The space itself resembles a theater (and is used for casual performances), but its main purpose is to present the menu of retailers to visitors like so many channels on a TV set. No doubt hoping to show the architecture rather than the performance, Portman took the photograph before business hours. Windows in the illuminated showrooms display mannequins dressed in the styles of the day, while discrete pairs of conversationalists punctuate the vast space of the empty mart. A man on the fourth terrace bends over a potted plant with a watering can. Another solitary figure occupies the central floor of the lowest terrace.

In these photographs (and, of course, we could add many more examples from the photographs by Iwan Baan presented in this volume), the Atrium seems to obey Diderot's imperative for the theater: "Act as if the curtain never rose!"[14] The Atrium is composed as if beholder and occupant alike were not there; the architecture is oblivious to the existence of any space produced outside its own, even as it accommodates (or ignores) every particularity. How, then, can this axiom of absorption, obliviousness, be reconciled with our previous conclusion that, in the dialectic of absorption and theatricality, Portman's work lands decidedly in the domain of the latter?

Fried's firm distinction between absorption and theatricality does not take full advantage of the developments of that discourse by Diderot in a text entitled "The Paradox of the Actor."[15] Consideration of that text suggests that the paradox of the actor is, too, the paradox of the Atrium. Diderot's paradox begins like this: "In my view, he [the actor, the artist] must have a deal of judgment. He must have in himself an unmoved and disinterested onlooker. He must have, consequently, penetration and no sensibility, the art of imitating everything, or, which comes to the same thing, the same aptitude for every sort of character and part."[16] *No sensibility?* In the 18th century feelings and emotions had become the very goal of acting. Actors who actually could feel their character's emotions were generally regarded as superior. Diderot's position is oppositional in extreme. He proposed that in order to evoke the strongest feelings in the audience, the good actor should feel nothing at all. Moreover, in order to play many characters with many emotions and, in general, in order to imitate everything, an actor needed to be entirely without qualities proper to the individual's own being.

In a close analysis of Diderot's "Paradox," Philippe Lacoue-Labarthe argues, "the paradox states of a *law of impropriety*, which is also the very law of mimesis: only the 'man without qualities,' the being without properties or specificity, the subjectless subject … is able to present or produce in general."[17] Or, paraphrasing Diderot's terms, the particular form of a work of art never interferes with the shapes art brings into appearance. It follows that a great work of architecture has no particular character proper to it. The aim, on the contrary, is a kind of unappropriated availability — an aptitude for presentation. Lacoue-Labarthe continues, then, to construct a general theory of mimesis that bears upon Diderot's formulation of "the art of mimicking everything," the "same aptitude for every sort of character and part."[18] There are two sorts of mimesis: first, there is a restricted form in which art imitates nature; this form is a reproduction or reduplication of what is already given, effected, and presented by nature. Second, there is general mimesis, which does not reproduce anything but rather "*supplements* a certain deficiency in nature, its incapacity to do everything, organize everything, make everything its work — *produce* everything."[19] This form of mimesis is a productive mimesis. Indeed, it is an imitation of nature as a productive force; it is art making up for human limitations by negating any particular character and presenting itself as pure potential. It is this form of productive mimesis that we find in the Atrium.

Returning now to our preliminary characterization and comparison of an architecture of absorption and theatricality, we can make the observation that many diverse and interesting tendencies in contemporary architecture continue the first order of mimesis. Biomimetic architecture, green design, parametric architecture, fractal geometric architecture, perhaps geometric architecture generally, all conform to a large extent to the ancient axiom of art imitating nature. Within the broader "absorptive" paradigm, this kind of mimesis uses "nature" both to establish consistency ("pictorial unity") and to support these architectural tendencies within a deeper aesthetic history proper to architecture's discipline. Portman's Atrium, however, follows the theater in its exemplification of a more general mimesis, a productive mimesis; that is to say, a presentation of something which was not yet given, not yet there, not yet present—a presentation of the aptitude for presentation. Which is to posit that the Atrium is theatrical in the sense of its general function of supplementation, which always falls to art (what Lacoue-Labarthe calls "the gift of mimesis"[20]). Read this way, a productive mimesis in Portman's Atrium preserves its theatrical quality without succumbing to the indictment of presentation levied by Diderot and Jameson. Our postmodern diagnosis, that the Atrium "produces everything," is thus viewed at an angle to these critics, an angle from which to redeem the vulgarity of its spectacle.

At first, Portman's Atrium (expansive, expedient, repetitive) appears at complete odds with Cohen's Lightfall (contained, considered, singular). However, both achieve absorptive unity, but in different ways. In the Atrium, we are not absorbed in precise reading, as in Cohen's, but made acutely aware of our own presence. We see ourselves in the tableau, while our precise location remains ever elusive. In the Atrium, the world itself becomes all-seeing, "a sensory world unto itself," and the field of representation announces a certain self-sufficiency; the world sees the beholder from all sides, as it were, while the beholder's perspective is blocked. Only this explains the euphoric effect of complete immersion and complete alienation. Absorbing the Atrium demands that *you* are absorbed into the Atrium. Held there, arrested by the Atrium's gaze, we realize that we ourselves have become an absorptive object.

1 Le Corbusier, *Toward an Architecture*, trans. John Goodman (Los Angeles: Getty Publications, 2007), 217.

2 Ibid., 216.

3 Ibid., 219.

4 Fredric Jameson, *Postmodernism, or, The Cultural Logic of Late Capitalism* (Durham: Duke University Press, 1991), 44.

5 Ibid., 14–15.

6 Kristi York Wooten, "How 1980s Atlanta Became the Backdrop for the Future," *The Atlantic*, March 30, 2015, http://www.theatlantic.com/entertainment/archive/2015/03/how-1980s-atlanta-became-the-backdrop-for-the-future/388769/.

7 Michael Fried, *Absorption and Theatricality: Painting and Beholder in the Age of Diderot* (Berkeley: University of California Press, 1980).

8 Ibid., 103–04.

9 Ibid., 17.

10 Ibid., 104.

11 Ibid., 76.

12 Ibid., 22.

13 Rice comments on his photographs: "The estrangement this process [of documenting the atrium spaces] precipitated was akin to but also quite different from Fredric Jameson's postmodern epiphany in the Bonaventure Hotel … The photographs don't 'capture' the space; one can't read them as an index of experience. If anything, they are kinds of incidents, prompts to further investigation of a condition that I had first tried to grasp experientially." Charles Rice, *Interior Urbanism* (London and New York: Bloomsbury, 2016), xii.

14 Quoted in Fried, *Absorption and Theatricality*, 95.

15 Denis Diderot, *The Paradox of Acting*, trans. Walter Herries Pollock (London: Chatto & Windus, 1883).

16 Ibid., 7.

17 Philippe Lacoue-Labarthe, "Diderot: Paradox and Mimesis," trans. Jane Popp, in Philippe Lacoue-Labarthe, *Typography: Mimesis, Philosophy, Politics*, ed. Christopher Fynsk (Cambridge, MA: Harvard University Press, 1989), 258–59.

18 Diderot, xii.

19 Ibid., 255.

20 Ibid., 259.

A Constant Vision in a World of Change

John Portman

The practice of architecture has changed a great deal in a relatively short time span. Dinosaur drafting tables have been rapidly replaced by computer stations, and the programs that run those computers have continually become more useful in a powerful way. What once took weeks can now be accomplished in hours.

Despite these rapid advances, the approach to architectural projects and the factors that drive design decisions remain rooted in the interpretation of basic human needs. Solutions through design can be the integrated expressions of function, purpose, and sensory experience, conceived in a holistic manner to create balance and harmony and to make perfect sense. Architecture was created for, and exists, to serve life.

Architects have a responsibility to society to direct growth in a way that is conducive to productive life. The environment must be intertwined spiritually as well as physically. It must be an environment dedicated to the dignity of man and his greatest ideals. Many can build, but it is the dedicated architect who breathes life and spirit into the creation of a place. The architect can go beyond the mere technical and fundamental aspects of building and create living architecture. That is how architects truly live up to their promise.

As the world evolves, the one constant is change. In architecture, as well as in life, man has the ability to create harmony. The architect is a spiritual interpreter of the physical world and, as such, is faced with complex problems. The speed of technological advances makes it necessary for an architect to broaden their personal vision and interest to properly prepare for the evolution of tomorrow's society.

Architects must make every facet of a building their own personal concern and interest. They, along with developers, must anticipate growth patterns. They must analyze needs before they occur. Only when architects are in front of growth can they influence its direction in a positive manner.

More pragmatically, architects must learn to be cost sensitive! They must be able to produce within programs and budgets. Architects can be idealists, yes, but practical idealists. There was a time when the concept of architects as developers was frowned upon because it was thought to be a conflict of interest. However, by understanding development, analyzing feasibility, and designing accordingly, an architect performs at the highest professional level on key with all of the notes! Knowledge should be embraced.

Architects must stretch their minds and learn as much as they can about everything. There is nothing outside the inclusive world of architecture. In order to interpret a society and produce for it, one must understand it. This gains importance as the world gets smaller and architects are tasked with creating design solutions in foreign lands. Only a deep and genuine understanding can produce meaningful solutions for an indigenous culture.

Having said that, people, wherever they live, are more alike than not. Human beings are creatures of nature, perceiving their environment through the five senses. Architects should strive to appeal more to the higher instincts of spiritual man and less to duplicating materialistic things; weave natural sensory experiences into the built environment; understand and comprehend the nuances of humanity intimately in order to create an environment that is more beneficial to people, more rewarding, and more pleasant to experience.

Architecture is not about preconceptions, it is about understanding relationship and context. A city is rarely built all at once. One building goes up, and another, then others, and the city evolves in an organic fashion. Just as nature takes a set of circumstances and evolves as needed, that is how architects should approach each set of circumstances. No project exists on its own. Absorb the bigger picture. Find not just what fits, but what enhances the situation. When architects can develop a design that arises out of its unique circumstances to better its surroundings and grow from that uniqueness, then they are making the contribution for which they have responsibility.

Imposing is having a preconception, seizing an opportunity and forcing it to work. That is wrong. Architecture is problem-solving.

Architecture is understanding the essence of things. First, identify and go straight to the heart of the matter, understand everything related to it, craft a solution; and from there, evolve it, just as nature would. Do that, and the design of the building will come out with irrefutable validity and integrity. It will serve its people, and stand the test of time.

Architects must direct their energies toward an environmental architecture, born of human needs and responding to vital physical, social, educational, and economic circumstances. While sustainability has become an industry buzzword, architects should embrace it as a personal responsibility. A sustainable society is one that meets the needs of the present without compromising the ability of future generations to meet their own needs. A healthy environment is intrinsically valuable and essential to a healthy society. Through the design of the built environment, architects have the opportunity to positively impact the natural environment and enhance the quality of human life. The exploration of evolving sustainable solutions will continually impact the physical expression.

There is a saying, a cliché perhaps, that states, "The more things change, the more they stay the same." It is so true. Architects today must keep abreast of ever-evolving technology. There are new materials, new techniques, and more choices than ever before. Yet, the issues architects face when designing a building are the same as they ever were. How can this design best serve the people who will use it? How will it improve their lives, enhance the lives of their neighbors, serve their community and generations to come? No matter what else changes, for an architect, the focus remains, as always, on people.

John Portman

John Calvin Portman Jr. was born in 1924 in Walhalla, South Carolina. He graduated from the Georgia Institute of Technology in 1950 and then went on to practice architecture in Atlanta.

His first significant project was the Atlanta Merchandise Mart, designed in 1957 and completed in 1961. Now renamed the AmericasMart Building 1, it was the initial building in what would evolve into the multiblock Peachtree Center, an extensive development of interconnected offices, hotels, commercial, and retail facilities. Besides creating a new type of interconnected business district, the center provided a haven from the heat and humidity of the Southern climate and brought life back to the streets of downtown Atlanta.

Portman's experience of this type of interior urbanism, including his innovative use of the atrium typology for hotel buildings, was replicated in many cities in the US and beyond. The Portman companies were among the first to establish a successful presence in China when it opened up to foreign architectural firms, and they have gone on to realize a significant number of large-scale architectural and urban projects in the country.

Combining architecture with development has played a significant role in John Portman's approach. From the very beginning, it was his deep understanding of the relationship between development and design that enabled him to transcend some of the orthodoxies and prevalent assumptions of architectural practice.

A less-known aspect of Portman's career is his dedication to art and culture. A prolific sculptor, he has designed a number of major pieces for his own buildings. These large and often spatially complex geometrical structures engage with and complement his architecture. Alongside the commercial success of the projects, Portman seems equally committed to exploring their role as elements that affect the life and experience of the people who use them. It is the uncommon and at times contradictory mixture of these interests that has made him an American icon.

Following Page: Dana Fine Arts Building at Agnes Scott College, Decatur, GA

There was a time when the concept of architects as developers was frowned upon, thought to be a conflict of interest. But to understand development, analyze feasibility, and design accordingly is an architect performing at the highest level. Knowledge is power and should be embraced.

JP

Portmanian Architecture

Preston Scott Cohen

Portmanian architecture is architecture characterized by the tropes that constitute the famed atrium hotels and office complexes of John Portman. These tropes include glass elevators as gondola lifts rotated onto the *z* axis; elevator shafts turned inside out to reveal their inner workings; lifts passing in and out of open space, solid concrete and glass tubes, and normal elevator shafts; transverse spatial sequences produced by escalators and ceremonial spiral stairs, and extended by sky bridges; hotel corridors open for viewing from afar; hyperarticulated balcony railings composed of horizontal and vertical patterns of porosity and plantings; the blurring of automobile and pedestrian thresholds; the suppression of the symbolic significance of entrances; the introduction of pavilions and sculptures as isolated architectural figures in the "plein air" of the atrium, a kind of interiorized urban space; revolving panoramic restaurants, invisible from the atrium and expressed on the outside as airborne devices anchored to the main building; the discrete articulation of reflective transparent components and textured opaque components on the exterior; the aggregation of vertically attenuated masses to produce wide office buildings; and the use of a cylindrical form as a means to reduce the apparent scale of already slender hotel annexes.

The tropes of Portmanian architecture are prevalent in the large-scale private developments designed by Portman's firm from the 1970s through the 1990s. Office complexes, malls, airports, and even museums emulated the immersive and urbanized architectural experience of the famed Portman hotel atrium, which aesthetic and political theorists like Fredric Jameson regarded as the apotheosis of postmodern space. Portman's tropes augmented and popularized the austere and brutal forms of modern architecture. Portman's work can effectively be characterized as a critique of modern architecture's commitment to moral principles—not least of which was the denunciation of excess, decoration, fashion, and other consumable, and thus passing, pleasures driven onward by capitalism.

In the 21st century, Portman's particular species of multilevel mixed-use development has continued to propagate, especially in rapidly urbanizing countries. However, its relationship to other types and scales of urban morphology has evolved significantly. Many Western cities have been recentralized. Automobiles, public transportation, ridesharing services like Uber, and, soon, self-driv-ing cars, have made it possible for the recreational amenities and conveniences of suburban living to be absorbed within dense urban environments, which provide far more desirable cultural and social experiences. Within this new hybrid, the Portman atri-um—conceived as aggregated units accessed by open balconies that border multilevel spaces—is no longer a suburban space transposed to the city. The atrium has become a far more complex system—attenuated, fragmented, and multiplied into a network of indoor and outdoor pedestrian promenades. These networked spaces integrate the full spectrum of hardscapes and landscapes, transportation and leisure, and support all uses (living, working, recreation). Alongside this tendency, the atrium type has been res-caled and adapted to the concept of the boutique: hotels and retail centers for small-scale vendors as opposed to megahotels and department stores. Meanwhile, many of the effects produced by the large-scale spatial manifestations of postmodernism have been usurped by handheld communication technologies.

The hypothesis of the studio was that the Portmanian tropes which play supporting roles in monumental atrium spaces can be recon-ceived as leading parts in an inside out and immersive urban-architectural ensemble. First, this required inverting the roles of the background and foreground elements. To that end, the stu-dents began by analyzing and manipulating the two types most definitive of the base condition of Portman buildings: the linear aggregation of rooms alongside balconies that act as corridors; and the cylindrical tower, which, as an object free of orientation, creates the experience of continuous space and movement that Portman wished to foster. The students analyzed the potential to use the aggregated rooms and circulation systems of these two types to generate spatial sequences. Many chose to introduce ramps, stairs, and promontories to accentuate the spectacle of public perusal. The elevator core was also reconsidered. It no lon-ger appeared as an autonomous entity that foiled the otherwise horizontal emphasis of Portman atriums, nor as a scaled down ver-sion of the cylindrical tower, but rather as an integral component with the distinctive capacity to introduce stability and interrupt the oblique and curving systems of lateral circulation.

The studio traveled to Atlanta to study Portman's buildings. After meeting with John Portman and visiting his houses in Atlanta and Sea Island, Georgia, the students began to recognize the signifi-cance of his goal to act as both a developer and architect to transform the city. The houses served as laboratories for experimentation in the generation of patterns of space that would allow the multiplication of a diversity of activities without having to compromise the economic advantages yielded by flexible planning. Portman's plan geometries embodied structural systems, as well as access and egress systems, producing innovative commercial spaces for marketing, office, retail, and hotel uses. The students debated the role of formal artistry versus the strategies by which space becomes profitable and as a result catalytic of economic and social change (with both positive outcomes and some questionable social consequences, such as the monopolization by global forms of capital at the expense of local businesses and residents).

For their own projects, the students were required to explore sites in their hometowns or other cities they had intimate and detailed knowledge of. They were asked to identify new ways to integrate the large-scale vertically structured atriums and cylindrical towers with small-scale horizontally disposed urban districts. In order to make their buildings much more porous and programmatically integrated with the horizontal contexts—and to overcome the monumental bases that so often pervade Portman projects—the students introduced new types of modulation along the edges of the taller structures. Whereas Portman's primary task was to segregate pedestrian and vehicular traffic while still providing the smoothest possible flow of cars in and out of garages, the students understood their priority to be the discovery of ways to support the meshing of different but interrelated pedestrian cultures for which the automobile was no longer the determining factor.

The ultimate aim of the studio was to use the tropes of Portmanian architecture to develop an architectural language that could be applied as a technique of urban design.

Transformational Studies

The studio began with a series of exercises. The first project was an adaptive transformation. In a uniform transformation, such as scaling, everything changes proportionally according to a consistent function, regardless of the make up of the internal elements. However, in an adaptive transformation, the integrity of the parts must be preserved during the distortion of the whole. This can result in internal proportional changes and, potentially, in significant interference of the whole by the parts.

As a starting point for exploration, a large-scale uniform distortion was applied globally to an existing Portman building. Then, internal adjustments were made to the building to compensate for the interruptions caused by the distortion, and to preserve its main organizational, sequential, and figurative aspects. Since these adjustments could not completely restore the building's coherence, further compensations were required, setting a process into motion.

In order that they could be read backwards, the transformations were thought of systematically. The transformations were required to have some parametric integrity, so that, if time allowed, a script might be built to generate them. In other words, certain relationships were required to be held constant while other relationships were allowed to change according to a consistent logic. The students were not asked to actually create parametric models but rather to understand the architectural language that they were developing in parametric terms. The constructed Rhino models were estimations of the end results of transformative operations. They were protoparametric buildings based on implicit formal relationships.

To begin their transformational investigations, the students were asked to select one of the following operations:

1. Distort the building globally.

This is a uniform operation, which at first is applied to the whole building indiscriminately. The operation could be a cage edit bending the building; or a 1D scale stretching the building (horizontally or vertically) or racking the building (into a parallelogram or, projectively, a trapezoid). Some rooms will have to remain close to their original state, while others will be allowed to transform more loosely. A room can only rack so far before it becomes unusable. The building could, as a whole, rack more than the rooms. The difference between rooms and the overall building shape may have to be resolved with poché. As the building bends, the facade may get longer on one side and shorter on the other. Certain programs that were on one side of the building may get pushed to the other. Perhaps certain programs that were previously embedded within the building can now reach the facade.

2. Shrink the building.

This involves decreasing the overall floor area of the building. As the area decreases, some rooms will be able to shrink easily. Other elements, like bathrooms, corridors, and stairs, will have more rigid, fixed sizes, particularly if the height of the building is preserved or increased. Some rooms will be demanding and need to maintain their shape. These rooms may end up pushing into other more malleable rooms, causing plan changes. The internal proportions of the building will, therefore, change adaptively in a manner that is not identical to the changing proportions of the exterior shape. If the exterior shrinks uniformly and the interior responds adaptively, then the exterior envelope may also become dislodged from the interior. In addition, the facade might have allegiances of its own, such as to symmetry, that will force it to behave differently than the interior, exacerbating these effects. At a certain point of shrinkage, some rooms will need to be removed to avoid forcing all the rooms to shrink. Once they are removed, gaps may be left in the building. These gaps will need to be closed so that the building remains knitted together.

3. Add to the inside of the building.

This could be a new function, a significant new room or destination, a new stair, a whole new circulation system, or even a new floor. The building will have to compensate for the addition of a new body inside of it. For example, if the addition is a new floor, the building must either increase in height or the floors must compress. Floors can only compress so far before they become unusable. In addition, it may not be wise to compress floors uniformly. Some areas may require height while others may not. Internal shearing may result. It will be necessary to determine whether the new element is an integral part of the original sequence or a separate, alien object. If the building is a tower, the addition of a floor will not disturb its organization. However, if the building is a museum, such a floor will undoubtedly disrupt the sequence. If the floor is an administrative level or a separate gallery, it may require its own circulation, and the original circulation may need to skip over it. However, if the circulation through the building is continuous, this new anomalous element will need to be incorporated as best as possible.

4. Change the building's shape.

This entails forcing the perimeter of the building into a new shape typology. For example, if the building is rectangular, fold it into an L shape. Does the building bend or break as it folds? Determine what happens at the fold point on the expanded corner and at the crunch. Once the building is distorted, compensate for the distortion on the interior by preserving some significant aspects of the building's organization while abandoning and transfiguring others. Determine which characteristics of the building's experience are relevant in the new configuration and which have been dramatically weakened by the distortion. Determine, too, which aspects of the interior can remain the same and which must change.

5. Tilt the building.

This involves sectionally modifying the building as though it were on a slope. As the building tilts, the floor plates will shear; circulation will either shear (producing stairs) or tilt (becoming ramps). To address the shearing, it will be important to determine where the floor plates are allowed to break. Furthermore, it may be necessary to add additional stairs to preserve connections in the buildings. How will the building make room for the addition of stairs? Can adjacent space simply be eliminated, or does the building need to compress, preserving its interior floor area? When tilting the corridors, it is essential to address what happens when ramps become too steep for walking. The building might be elongated to add more length for the ramps. Alternatively, the ramps might fold to acquire more length. This will force them to take up more space in plan, and may even force them to puncture the exterior. If they puncture the exterior, how does the envelope/facade compensate for or preserve its integrity? Perhaps its surface area can remain the same despite the new opening, causing folding or wrinkling to occur.

6. Shear the building.

This involves sectionally displacing the interior of the building while preserving the exterior. The effects of the interior transformation will be similar to those of the tilted building. However, on the exterior, the facade will have the responsibility to try to hide the internal transformation. New relationships must be found between the apertures on the exterior and the rooms on the interior.

7. Turn the building.

This entails shifting the entrance or moving it to a whole new side of the building. The interior sequence will have to adjust to reach the new entrance and either preserve as much of the original experience as possible or overcompensate by producing a new experience. How does the building negotiate between its two orientations? Does it try to hide or exaggerate the change that has taken place? In addition, the new circulation system will obviously intersect with spaces in the building. These spaces will need to be moved out of the way.

8. Bend the building into a U shape.

This is similar to bending a building, except it also forces the building into a new typology.

9. Change the building into a loop.

This involves connecting the entrance of the building with the end of the internal sequence. First the building will need to be elongated and bent or folded. Once the loop has been made, determine a new way to enter the building and modify the sequence accordingly.

10. Locally scale a piece of the building.

This involves choosing either an exterior element, such as a window, or an interior piece of the program, and then changing its size. Determine what happens to the surrounding parts of the building as the element changes size. If it is a window, do all parts of the window increase uniformly in scale? Maybe the amount of facade surface area has to remain constant, causing buckling or creasing. Maybe the windows around it move away to preserve the distance. If windows move, do they drag along rooms on the interior? If it is a room, can the other rooms compress around it, or will rooms push out of the building in order to preserve their area?

11. Invert the building.

This requires turning the building inside out or outside in. The building will now have a facade type condition on the inside and all the rough internal rooms and circulation exposed on the outside. Make this new configuration into a meaningful building by determining how it can repack itself and form a complete sequence. Create a new facade for the building. What is the relationship of the new facade to the original facade? Is there a new space inside the old envelope? What is the role of this space in the sequence?

12. Change the structural system.

How does the building respond?

13. Cross the building.

This involves producing a new intersection in the circulation sequence. It is similar to looping the building except that the intersection occurs not at the entrance but at some other point along the sequence. Imagine that two corridors on different floors were modified sectionally and forced to cross each other. As they crossed, one corridor would need to be displaced planimetrically. What would happen to the rooms along the way? The rooms could probably decrease in height up to a certain point, but eventually another solution would be required. What type of space would be produced at the intersection? Alternatively, the entire building could be changed to migrate sectionally—enough that it gets under itself at one point. A new space could be produced at the cross point.

You got to believe in yourself. You got to have confidence, faith.
You got to have conviction.
You got to have discipline.
And you got to learn how to focus, and to prioritize.

JP

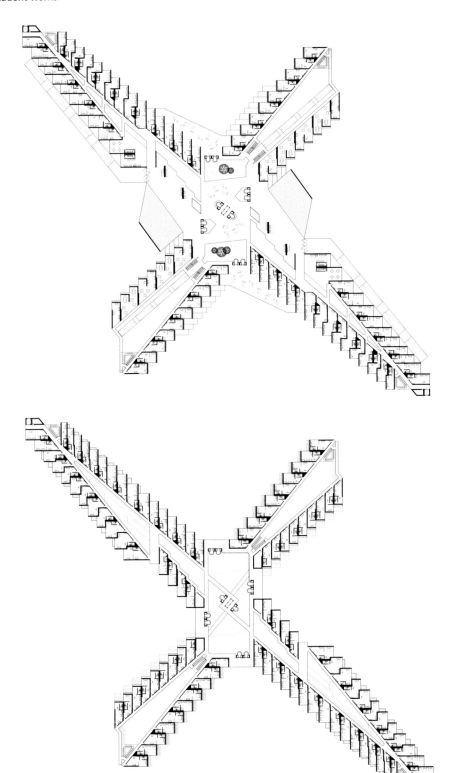

Inverse Corners
Sicong Ma, Seattle, WA

John Portman's hotels—the type in which a central atrium often sits on top of a podium floating above the ground—can be interpreted as a refusal to connect with the degraded urban context of modern American cities. According to Fredric Jameson, the atrium and the public space within the podium attempts to substitute itself for the outside world in order to create a better place for the people living there.

Inverse Corners / Urban Crossroad challenges this attitude of turning away from the urban context; it attempts to reactivate a flat, left-as-it-is parking lot in front of CenturyLink Field in Seattle. Vertical circulation cores serve as pivotal points and break the rigid rectangular arrangement of rooms and corridors into a

series of L-shaped bars that are cranked around such points. When combined with the fixing force from the in-room plumbing system, which stays anchored through the height of the building, the building generates a serial transformation of room sizes and double- and single-loaded corridor situations.

On a larger scale, the L-shaped volumes are rearranged so that the enclosed interior atrium is opened up into a series of four semi-embraced exterior public spaces that activate the site and are in dialogue with their surrounding context. This new central "common ground" is elevated, but still accessible by the ramps from all four orientations and thus integrated with the hotel lobby on the street level.

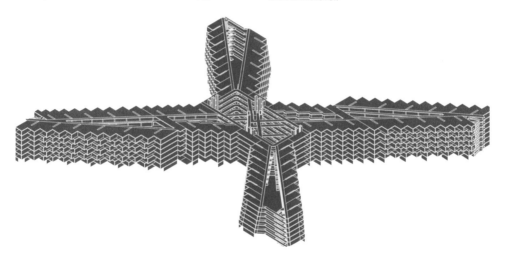

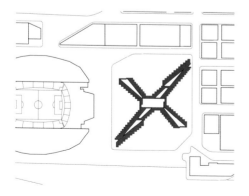

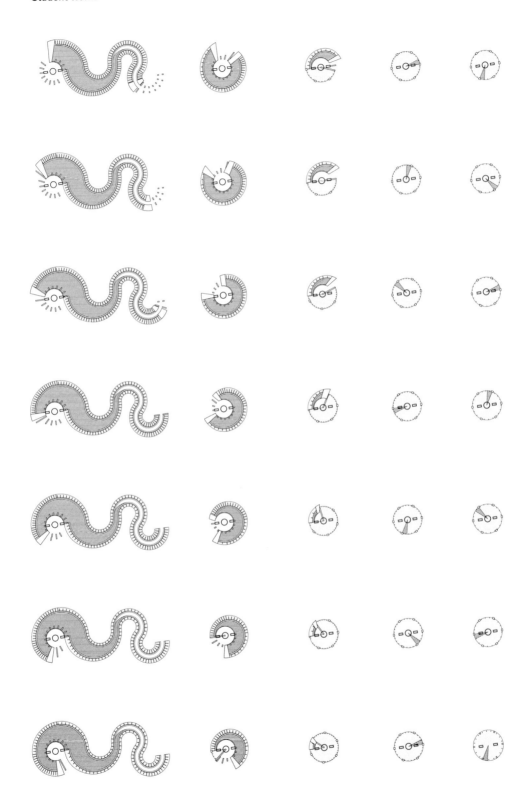

Port City
Patrick Baudin, Chicago, IL

Port City anticipates the death of the hotel as we know it. More and more, individuals are becoming empowered to engage in commerce through online marketplaces. Port City is envisioned as a new kind of hotel-residence for homeowners who rent out their space on a short-term basis. The building's structure and organization is directly tied to this programmatic model.

Port City is sited next to Bertrand Goldberg's River City complex in Chicago. Portman's and Goldberg's buildings share several traits: atriums, primary forms, and ornamental facades and details. Port City is conceived

as a long building, compressed to a t on a short site, and forced to negotiate the languages of the two architects. River City sets the Port City plan in motion, using the behavior of the arc to control both the building's compression and transitions between its three main sections.

The first section partially completes Goldberg's original River City plan, which included a series of fragmented S-shaped buildings whose arrangement formed a continuous, linear exterior atrium. The second section is a more Portman-like interior atrium that curves, slopes, and bends back around itself to eventually become the third section, a cylindrical office tower. The tower is envisioned as an office typology designed to serve Chicago's startup culture, which is characterized by the rental of shared open office space by individuals and small groups. Port City's new office typology adopts a circular plan that is made efficient by this novel type of work, since it is unbound by the partitioning and furniture constraints of the traditional multitenant office tower.

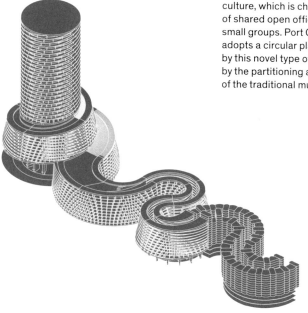

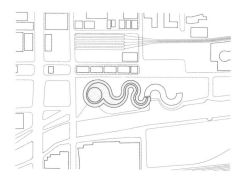

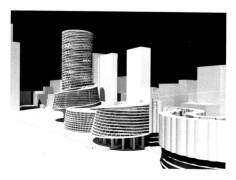

Playa Portal
Katie MacDonald, Playa Vista, CA

Playa Portal—a mixed-use complex containing a hotel, apartments and townhouses, and retail space—forms an urban corridor that connects to the 1940s hilltop suburban neighborhood of Westchester, California. A gradient is created, with housing-unit types transitioning from the single-family home to the hotel room.

Building on the lineage of John Portman, the complex features people movers in the form of elevators, landscape elements in the form of a public promenade and trail, and sunken-podium conference spaces. Movement is choreographed as a spectacle, with residents and guests perched on balconies and terraces, from which pedestrians and cars can be viewed. Order and variety are achieved simultaneously, as generic hotel units rotate and morph to view the city. Automotive circulation connecting the urban axis of Campus

Center Drive and the suburban axis of Firebrand Street is sunken below a green promenade of trails, recreation spaces, and seating areas. At the bottom of the bluff, the public corridor spills out into a large plaza with retail shops and pop-up space for food trucks, concerts, markets, and other gatherings.

Linking two neighborhoods that are close in proximity but distinct in cultural context, Playa Portal employs public space as means of fostering social diversity. The project upends the dependence on driving and creates a new model of hotel for modern-day Los Angeles.

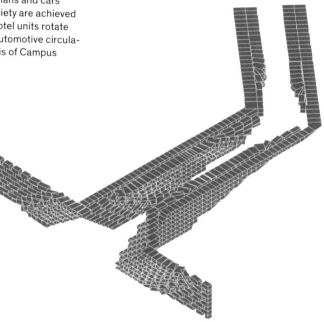

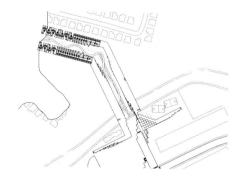

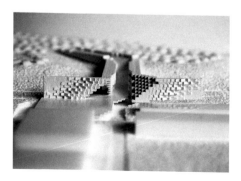

Triangular Localism
Yu Chen, San Francisco, CA

John Portman believes that "timelessness" in architecture is achieved through classical references, namely symmetry and pure geometry. He is interested in the duality of common citizens being both the audience and the performer in the public realm. Thus, his architecture aims to achieve theatricality.

The emotional vertigo one undergoes in any of Portman's hotel lobbies, the ability to openly watch and be watched in many of the terraced spaces, and to seize 360 degrees of a city and yet remain strangely uninvolved in his revolving restaurants, is evidence of architect's desire to shape people's experience through design. These personal ideologies of space and a strong belief in the power of space result in a Portmanian formula that is exclusive yet universally applicable.

The triangular site is right off of Embarcadero Street, across from the Pier. Due to high property values, housing and density demands, and changing hotel trends, the building's major programs include hotel rooms in its western wing and duplex residential units on the eastern side. Elevating the hotel and residential areas are the hotel lobby and marketplace. The building responds directly to the tricky triangular site with extremely tailored arrangements of five different modules. Shifting and stepping, these five 400-square-foot modules allow each hotel and residential unit to have an outdoor balcony and corner windows that grant views of the water and the city.

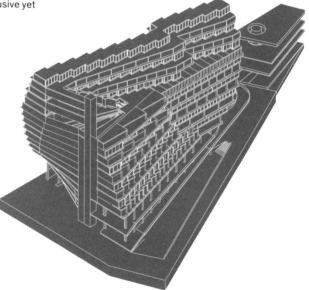

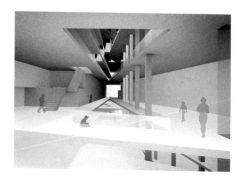

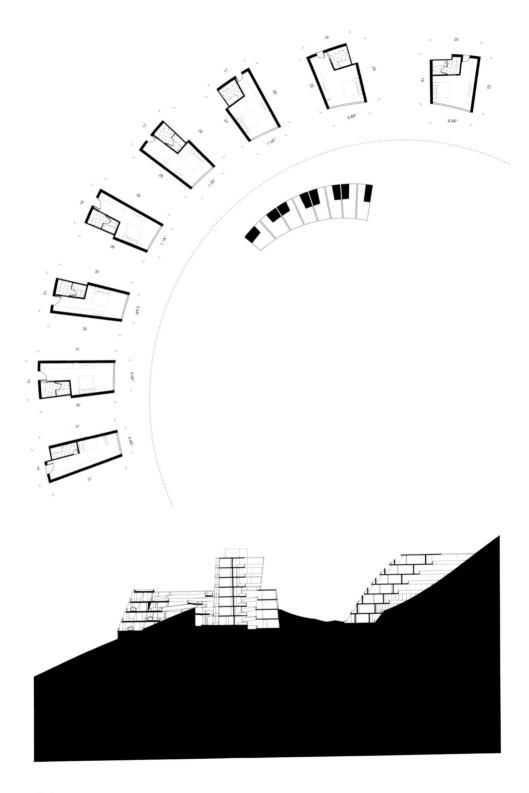

Craterscape
Yinjia Gong, Volcano, HI

The diversity present in a Portman hotel atrium creates an interior urbanscape. By opening up the inside of the atrium, the space gains visual access to the landscape. Views of this landscape drive the transformation of the rooms. The hotel is sited within a dead volcano crater. The depression of the topography gives the site a peaceful atmosphere.

My main concern in this project was the view of the inside landscape. Inserted into the landscape, the architecture merges with its surroundings. Panoramic views are created by arranging the rooms in different directions. A study of the typology started from the location and organization of the corridors inside the plan. Instead of putting the corridor along the

inside or outside wall, or in the middle of the cylindrical hotel tower, the corridor is placed on both sides of the wall. This allows for multiple directions of rooms within a single building. By cutting the cylinder in the middle to open the atrium to the outside landscape, the rooms face different views.

The cylinder follows the contours of the topography, embracing the convex and inserting it into the concave. Changing the location of the corridor allows the rooms to have the best view into the crater. When the building is inserted into the concave, the corridor is on the side closest to the concave, allowing the rooms to face the landscape.

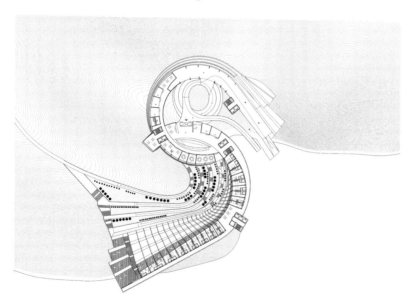

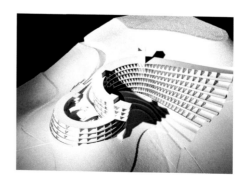

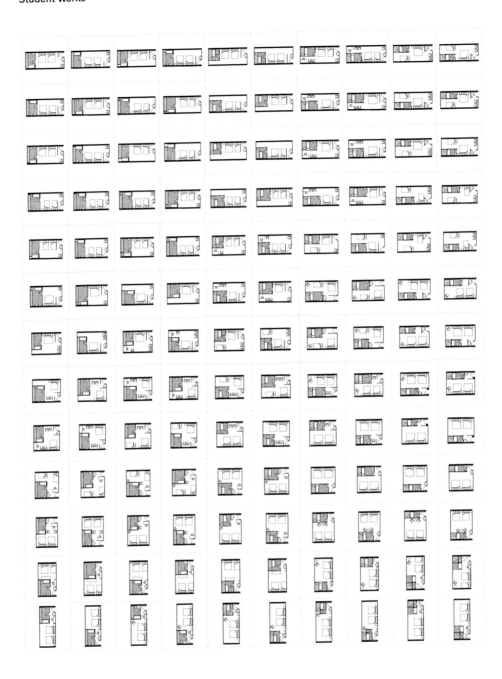

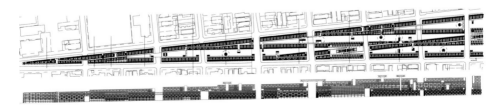

French Variation
Jaewoo Chon, New Orleans, LA

The city of New Orleans imposes unavoidable constraints on Portmanian architecture, which typically prefers to be siteless. Originating from the French land subdivision system, the city's historic downtown is based on a radial street grid projecting toward the Mississippi River. Precisely because of its salient urban fabric, New Orleans resists architectural monuments.

Instead of a Portmanian adaptation that attempts to "circumscribe a square into a triangle," the proposal utilizes the logic of the New Orleans grid itself, exploiting its irregularities. The street grid of New Orleans contains consistent triangular wedges, indivisible leftovers of its radial system. While these sections of the city currently lay mute and maintain a uniform urban quality, an application of Portmanian language provides such conditions with special urban characteristics.

The project utilizes the linear procession of rooms — the basic component of Portmanian architecture, consistent in almost every one of Portman's urban projects — as a generator. The linear procession of rooms in Portmanian architecture is most often static; it is limited

to the formation of discrete prismatic volumes that are organized to make voids and basic compositions, or rolled up to create cylindrical towers. The project introduces a gradual typological attenuation to the static linearity: while its area is maintained, the width and the depth of rooms gradually shift. Rooms that were completely uniform now consist of different interiors based on the gradual dimensional difference.

The logic eventually introduces typological variations: a single-loaded progression gradually shifts to double-loaded to duplex to atrium to courtyard. (An entire architectural genealogy in one building ...) As the strand continues to grow, it splinters off to create new strands, simulating the lot subdivision of New Orleans. The phylogenic structure is a radical reinterpretation of the existing city grid.

Boston has the Hancock. New York has the Flatiron. New Orleans adopts the Portmanian French Variation.

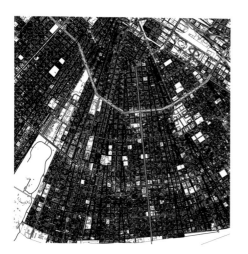

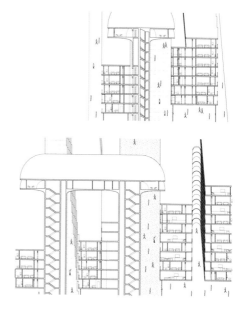

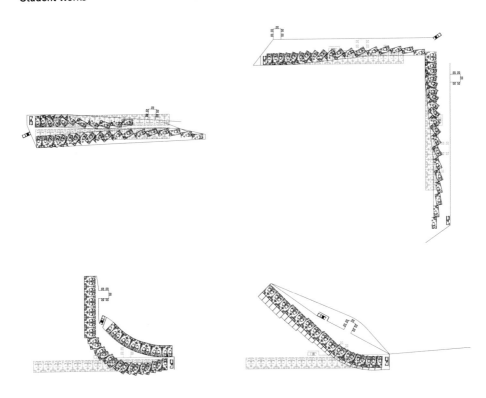

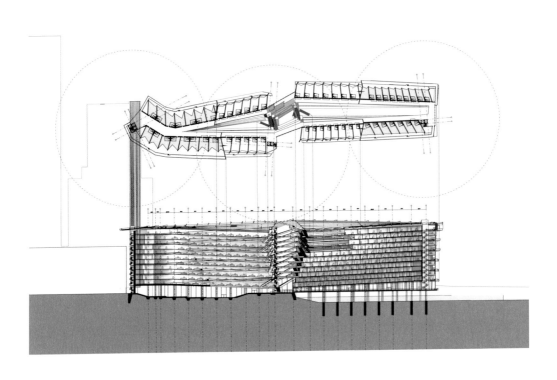

Contiguous Inclinations
Michael Piscitello, Detroit, MI

This exercise looks at architectural space as the function of an interior logic unfolding at an infrastructural depth. The resonance of this unfolding throughout reconstitutes programmatic typologies and urban identities that are coincidental with the site. These architectural explorations are aimed at expanding the repertoire of mutations in the the type of built environment that Fredric Jameson said we would need to grow new organs to understand.

This is a new hyperspace, one which examines architecture's urban identity as a function of its interior logic, as well as the relationship between architecture, infrastructure, and hybrid space.

Inspired by the sculptural helical stairs of John Portman's Embarcadero Center in San Francisco, this project seeks to integrate circulation at the infrastructural depth of the building as a driver for new programmatic typologies and urban identity. Architecturally, the building performs as a large helical stair, the landings of which have been elongated and charged with horizontally contiguous and vertically alternating hotel and apartment spaces. Global distortions agitate the individual rooms, which act as high-resolution fibers and allow the global transformations and spatial ordering of the interior to resonate on the textural exterior of the building.

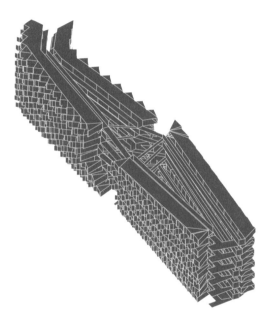

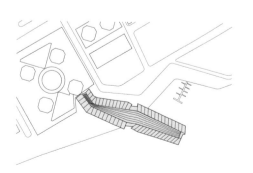

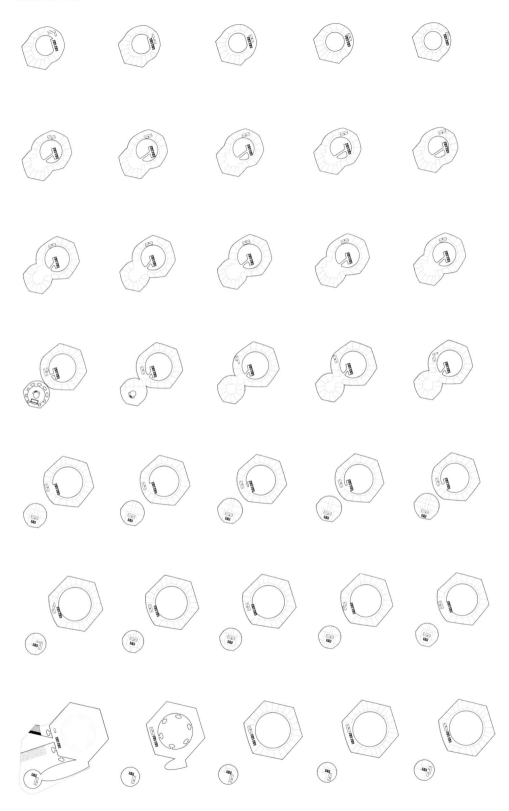

Houston Heel

Wen Wen, Houston, TX

Starting from an exploration of the spatial organization of cylindrical towers, the project explores the possibility and implications of blending radial and parallel spatial strategies. By combining these blended floor plans with a leaning atrium, the resulting tower creates a unique system of egress which "travels" around the core of the tower.

The massing results from folding a cone twice. This creates an annex and an external check-in lobby with escalators linking the two separate buildings. The annex, while linked to the main building volumetrically, embeds within itself a separate set of vertical circulation and egress (thus, in effect, functioning as its own building). Similar to Portman annexes, which are accessed through the main building, the annex here is accessed through the larger volume.

The three-step procession from drop-off vestibule to lobby to room is further reinforced: vehicular drop-offs occur on the ground level (linked to the greater urban context); the lobby is located in the smaller cone, one level below ground; and rooms in both buildings are accessed through the check-in lobby. The relationship between building and city is inverted by suppressing the podium under-ground. While Portman buildings have generally "turned their back" on the city, with a monolithic podium containing the atrium, an external outdoor atrium formed by the two separate vol-umes and shaded by their intersecting geometry opens up the ground floor and gives it back to the city.

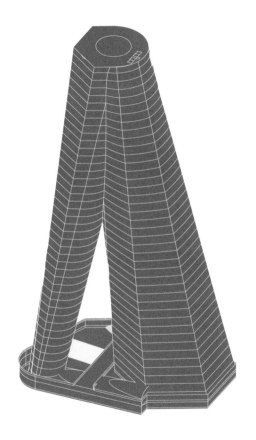

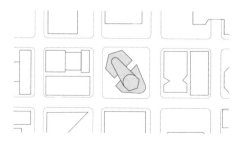

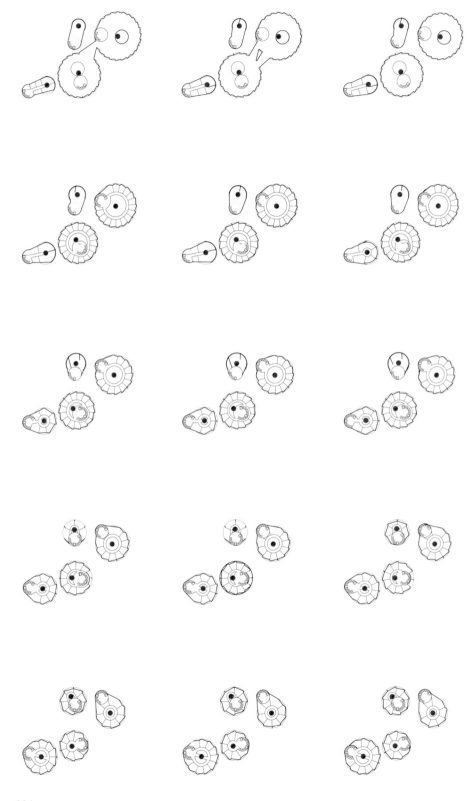

Pittsburgh, Grafted
Ranjit John Korah, Pittsburgh, PA

Pittsburgh, Grafted explores the capitalization of conventionally unusable land in the heart of downtown — the leftover scars of car-centric modernist planning. The mixed-used development of four towers contains a hotel, conventional and flexible office space, a public atrium for recreation, and, in anticipation of Pittsburgh's growing relevance in tech and education industries, a data center.

Following an exploration of Portman's three primary cylindrical towers, this project examines the spatial, textural, and formal conditions that can be created by morphologically transforming the typical cylinder. The analysis includes tapering, tilting, and stretching the cylinder (through a multitude of translations) in order to produce visual effects and spatial propositions that never existed in Portman's own designs. These towers both complement and antagonize one another in order to define and sculpt vertical parallax in the airspace of the site. Each pair of towers defines a perfectly parallel moment that is only captured from specific vantages.

By stretching the cylinder's base away from the core in order to accommodate the narrow parcel of land, a secondary volume is defined in the mediated space between the tapering cone and the core. These resulting voids, surrounded in glass and welcoming a visual connection to the hypertrophic environment directly outside, present themselves as atria inherently different from the insular and exclusive Portman atrium.

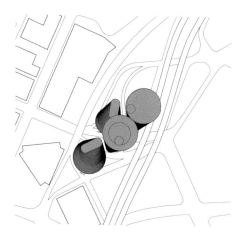

Hong Kong Split
Matthew Conway, Hong Kong, China

Portman seeks to generate architecture that creates autonomous urban environments. As Rem Koolhaas points out, this is done without inhibition, opposition, or influence; without the messy conditions, complexities, irregularities, and densities inherent in urbanism, creating an irreverence toward infrastructure. While critiques of Portman's work create an image of megalomaniacal insertions into urban downtowns, the architecture, when exploded into its elements, provides precedents for relating to the urban.

This project focuses on two tower types developed by Portman: the smaller cylindrical towers of the Westin Bonaventure in Los Angeles and the cylindrical annex to the Hyatt Regency Atlanta. Whereas in the Hyatt the elevator is in the center of the tower, in the Bonaventure the elevator is detached, acting as a bridge between towers. However, one may reimagine this disconnection as providing the possibility of connecting to urban elements as well. Furthermore, the mediation between these two types allows for a continuous architecture that has the ability to connect and relate to urban infrastructure. Unlike Portman's inward-looking architecture, this project has the ability to integrate into an urban context and absorb its complexities.

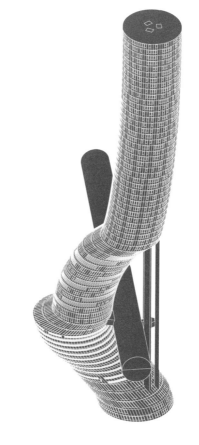

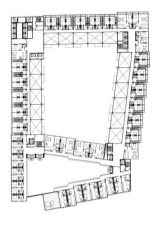

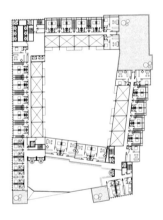

Port Manhattan
Harsha Sharma, New York, NY

The project explores the concept of a city within a city by the imbrication of hotel and housing programmatic elements within one building. The building connects to the urban landscape at the residential level, and the hotel element responds to the metropolitan skyline of New York.

Compared to Portman projects, which are introverted and as such could be situated on any site without any connection to the city, the building is sensitive to its context. To avoid having a dead base, the building responds to the bridge and tries to exploit the space below it rather than just above it. The sloped roof becomes the landscape for the hotel rooms and directs views towards the river. At the higher level, the tower sits on this new eroded stepping ground; it is connected to the city at an urban level since the rooms do not look at the undercroft of the bridge. The tower is situated at an ambiguous congruence, and the rest of the building is both an object and part of the overall form.

The eroded northeast corner opens up and connects back to the city. The courtyard engages the residential neighborhood. The interior atrium is shared by the hotel and housing, adding to the traditional Portmanian vocabulary by defining an atrium that acts as a public space on multiple dimensions.

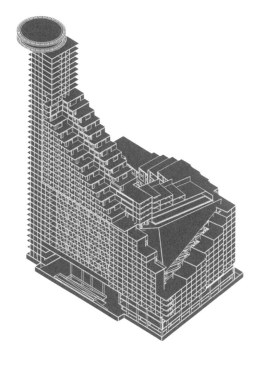

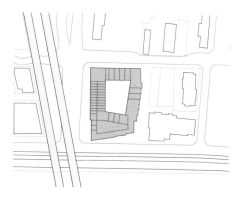

I talk about doing things holistically. I designed furniture, lighting fixtures. I even designed cocktail uniforms for the gals serving drinks at Midnight Sun. Somebody had to design them. Don't laugh at this, it's the truth.

JP

AmericasMart Building 3
Atlanta, GA

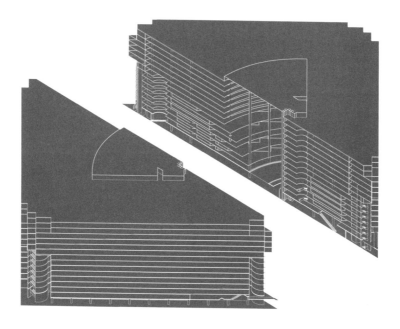

Emory University Student Center
Atlanta, GA

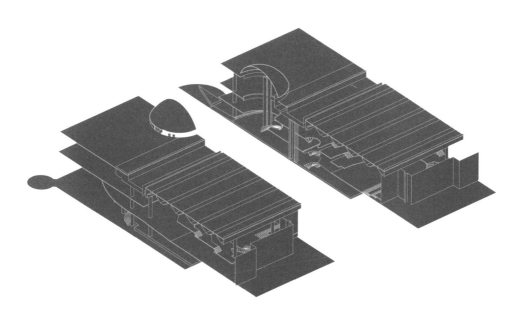

Atlanta Marriott Marquis
Atlanta, GA

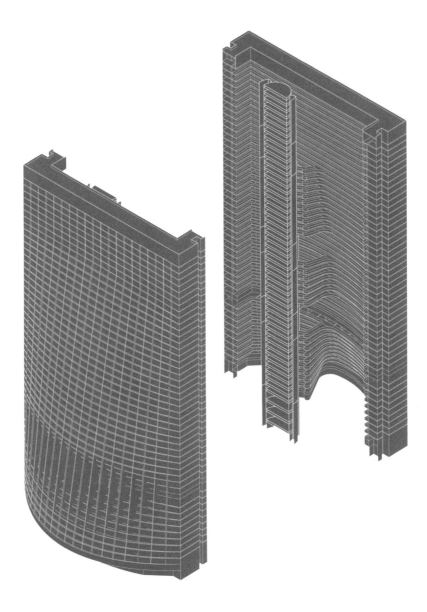

New York Marriott Marquis
New York, NY

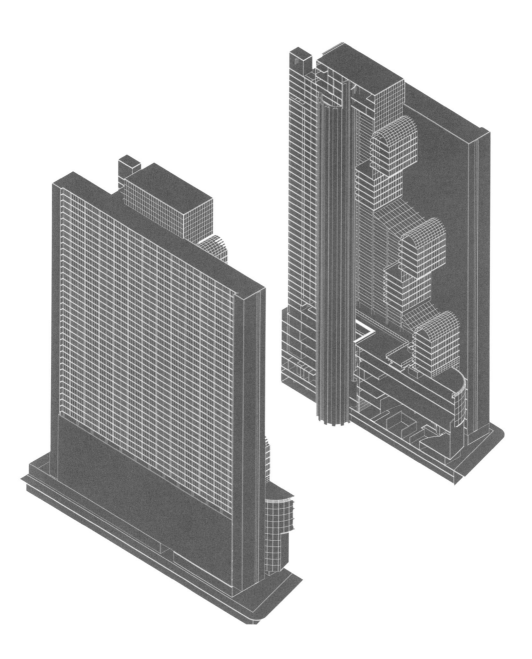

Four Embarcadero Center
San Francisco, CA

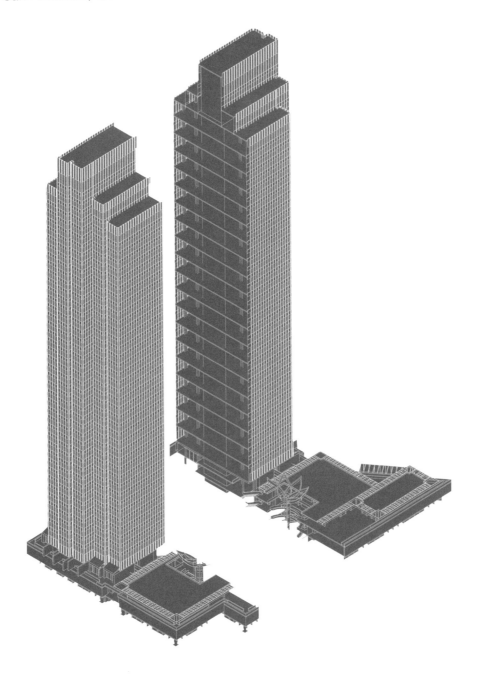

Hyatt Regency San Francisco
San Francisco, CA

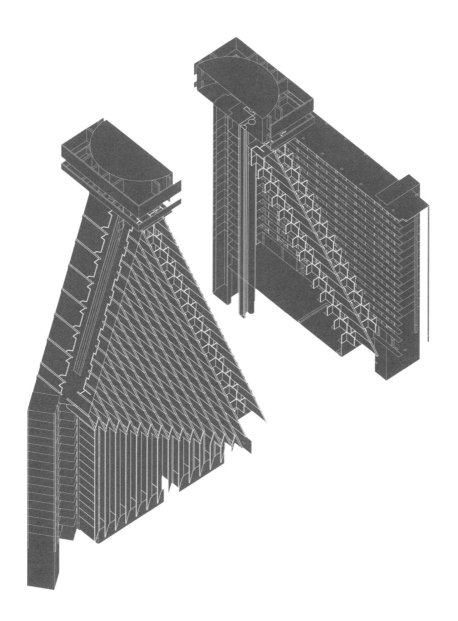

Hyatt Regency O'Hare
Chicago, IL

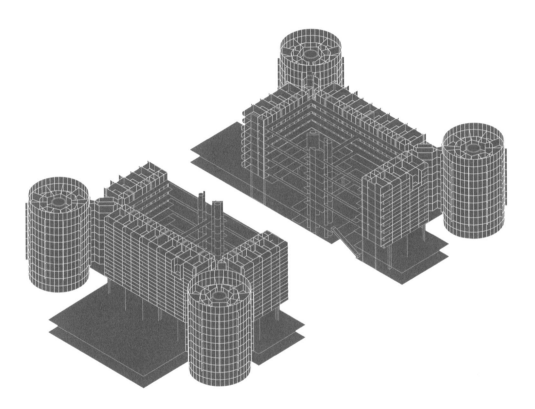

Westin Bonaventure
Los Angeles, CA

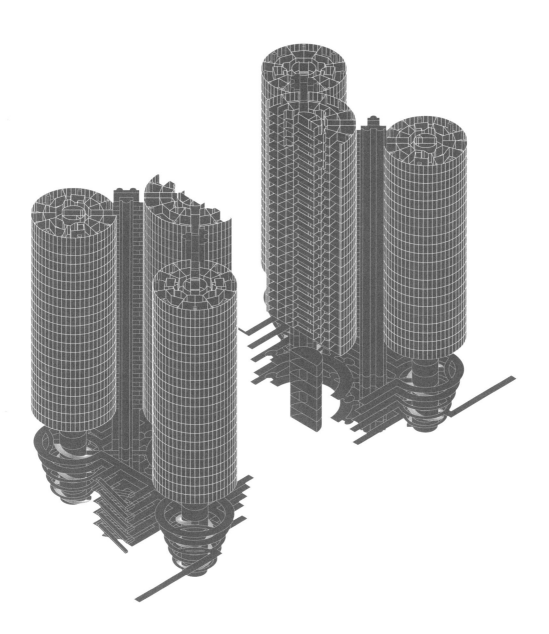

Westin Peachtree Plaza
Atlanta, GA

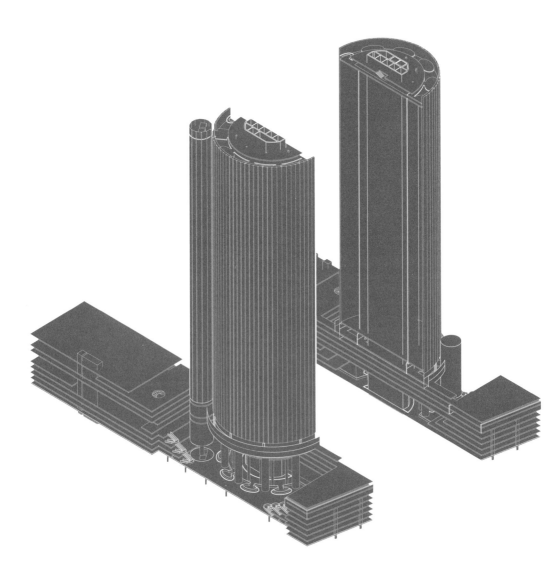

Renaissance Center
Detroit, MI

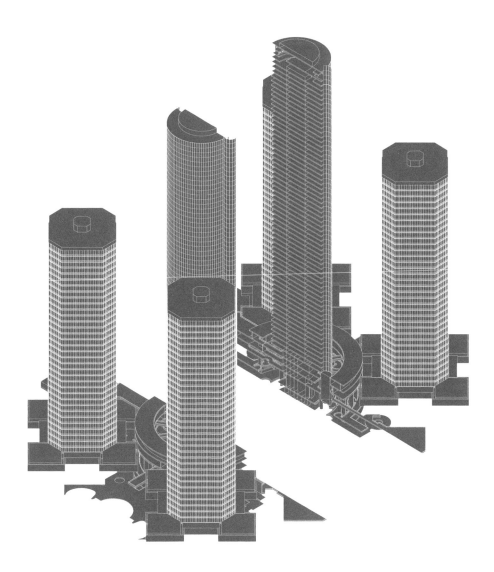

Architecture is not only a question of sight, it's a question of feel. Without even thinking, you say, "Well, that feels good. That feels great."

JP

Podium Program

Renaissance Center, Detroit, MI

Retail
Hotel
Conference
Office
Back of House
Restaurant

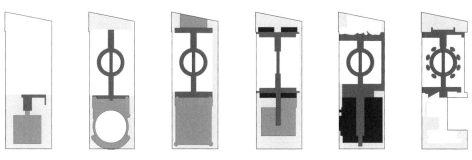

Westin Peachtree Plaza, Atlanta, GA

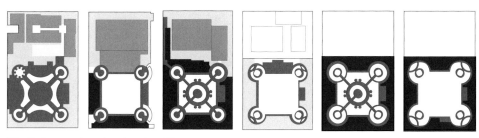

Westin Bonaventure, Los Angeles, CA

Cylindrical Hotel Lobbies

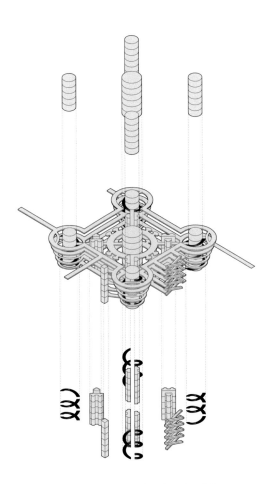

Westin Bonaventure, Los Angeles, CA

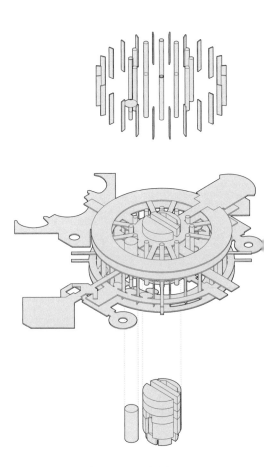

Renaissance Center, Detroit, MI

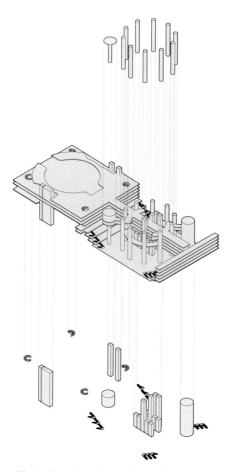

Westin Peachtree Plaza, Atlanta, GA

Revolving Restaurants

- ● Vertical Circulation
- ● Dining / Cocktail Lounge
- ● Bar
- ● Show Kitchen
- ● Circulation
- Back of House

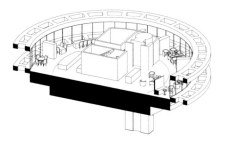

Polaris, Hyatt Regency Atlanta, Atlanta, GA

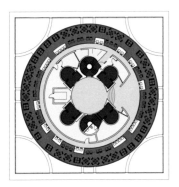
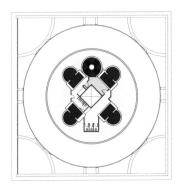

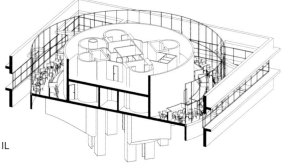

Ventana, Hyatt Regency O'Hare, Chigaco, IL

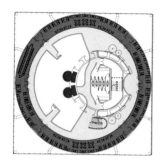
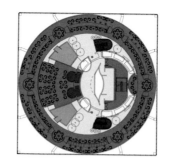
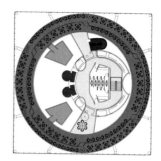
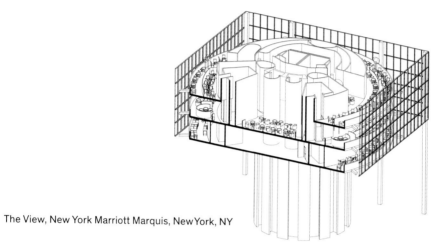

The View, New York Marriott Marquis, New York, NY

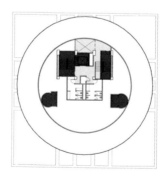
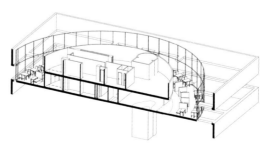

Equinox, Hyatt Regency San Francisco, San Francisco, CA

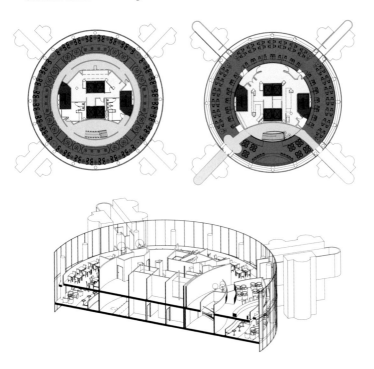

Bonavista, Westin Bonaventure, Los Angeles, CA

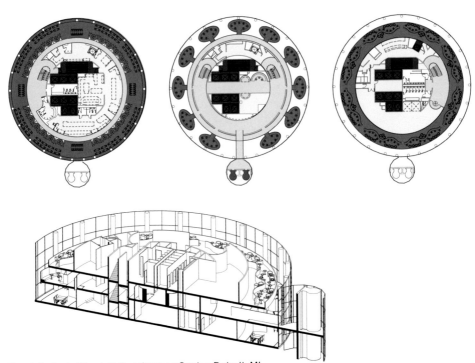

Coach Insignia, Marriott, Renaissance Center, Detroit, MI

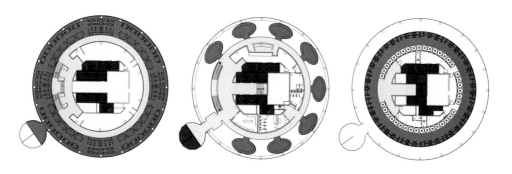

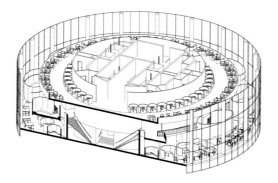

Sun Dial, Westin Peachtree Plaza, Atlanta, GA

● Vertical Circulation
● Dining / Cocktail Lounge
● Bar
● Show Kitchen
  Circulation
  Back of House

Egress Corridors

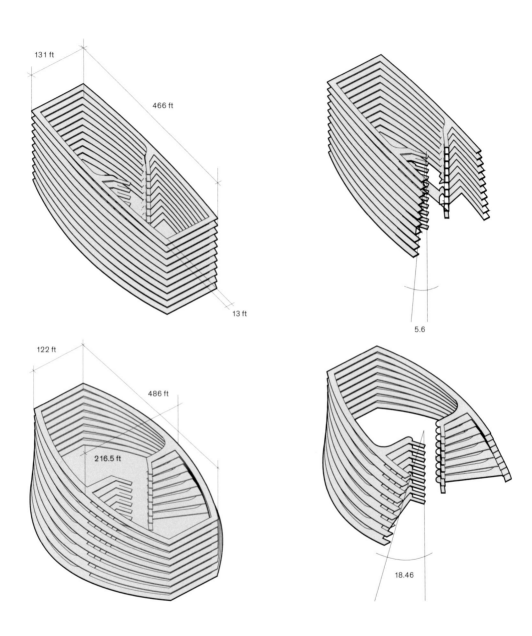

131 ft

466 ft

13 ft

5.6

122 ft

486 ft

216.5 ft

18.46

Atlanta Marriott Marquis, Atlanta, GA

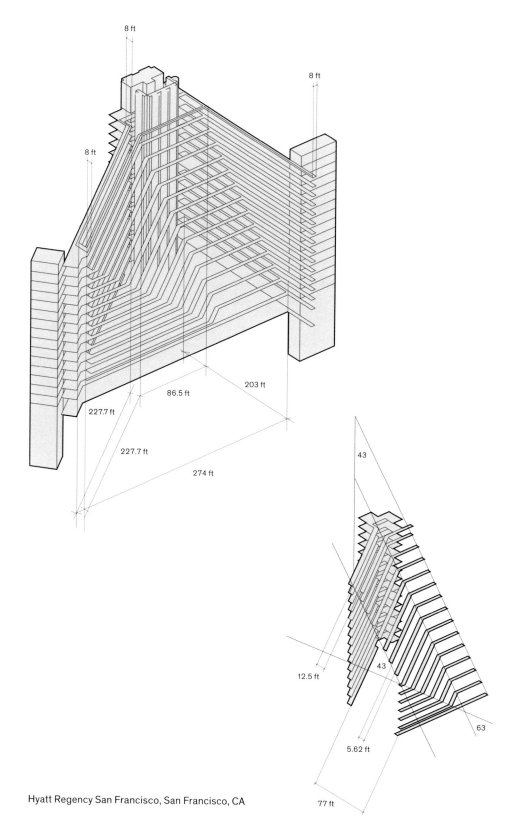

8 ft

8 ft

8 ft

203 ft

86.5 ft

227.7 ft

227.7 ft

274 ft

43

43

63

12.5 ft

5.62 ft

77 ft

Hyatt Regency San Francisco, San Francisco, CA

Facade Articulation

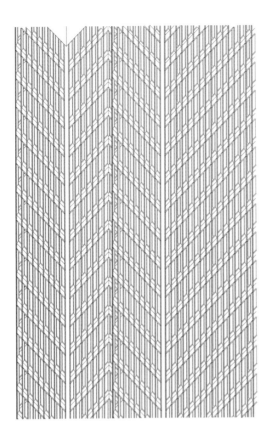

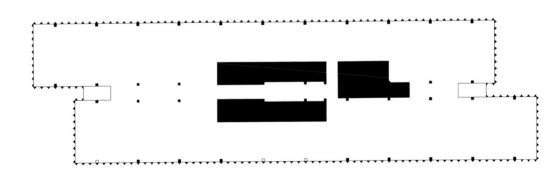

Peachtree Center, Atlanta, GA

0	20	40	80 ft

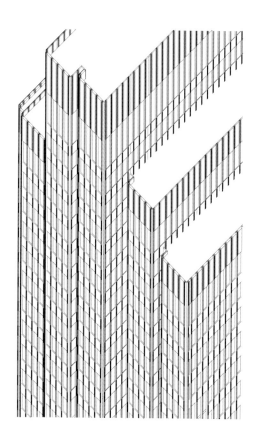

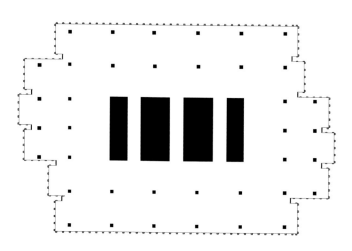

Embarcadero Center, San Francisco, CA

0   20   40   80 ft

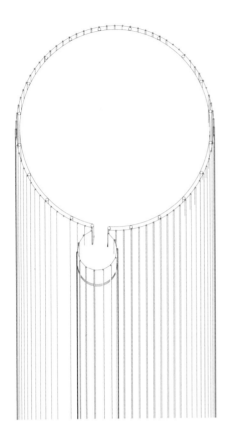

Westin Peachtree Plaza, Atlanta, GA

0   20   40   80 ft

Building Textures

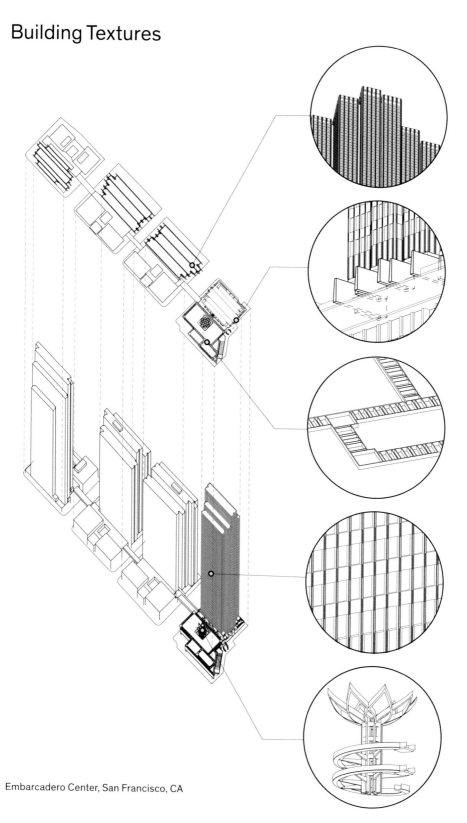

Embarcadero Center, San Francisco, CA

Facade Systems

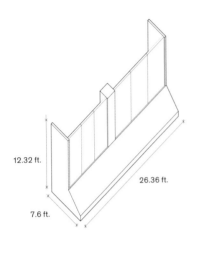

12.32 ft.

26.36 ft.

7.6 ft.

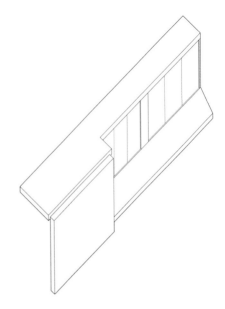

New York Marriott Marquis, New York, NY

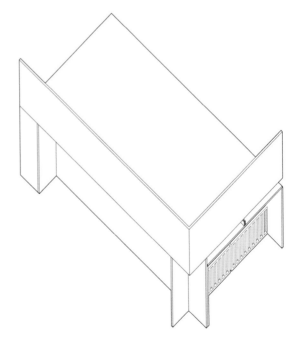

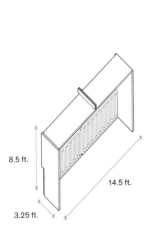

8.5 ft.

14.5 ft.

3.25 ft.

Hyatt Regency Atlanta, Atlanta, GA

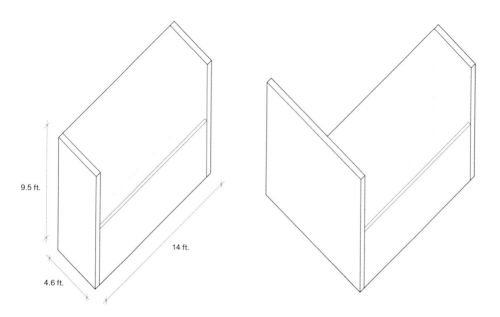

9.5 ft.

14 ft.

4.6 ft.

Hyatt Regency O'Hare, Chicago, IL

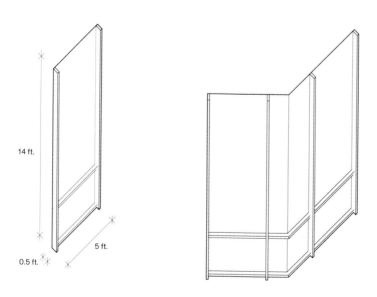

14 ft.

5 ft.

0.5 ft.

Renaissance Center, Detroit, MI

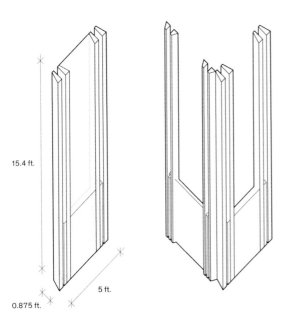

Embarcadero Center, San Francisco, CA

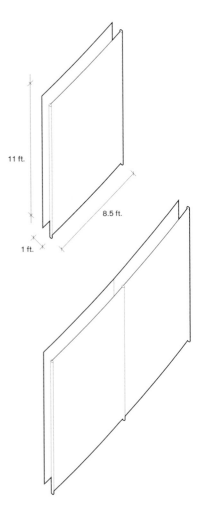

Westin Peachtree Plaza, Atlanta, GA

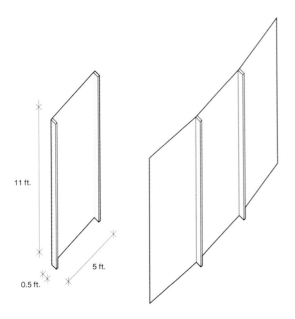

Westin Bonaventure, Los Angeles, CA

Parking

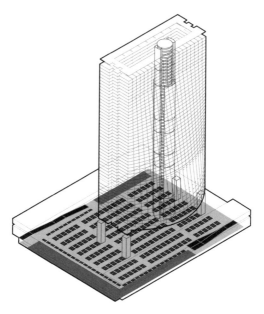

Atlanta Marriott Marquis, Atlanta, GA

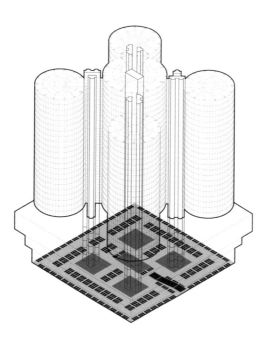

Westin Bonaventure, Los Angeles, CA

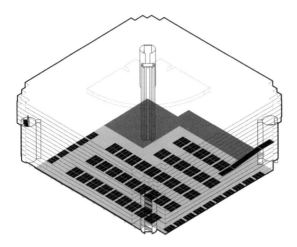

AmericasMart Building 3, Atlanta, GA

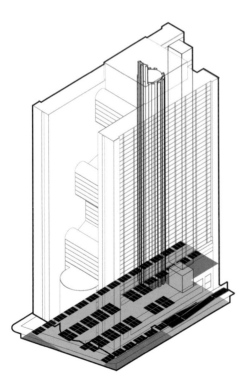

New York Marriott Marquis, New York, NY

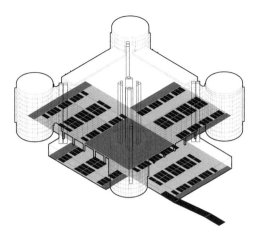

Hyatt Regency O'Hare, Chicago, IL

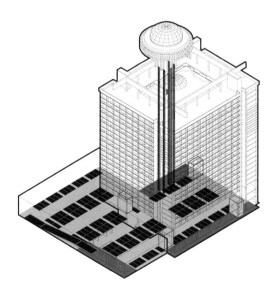

Hyatt Regency Atlanta, Atlanta, GA

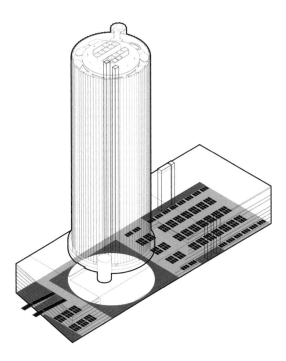

Westin Peachtree Plaza, Atlanta, GA

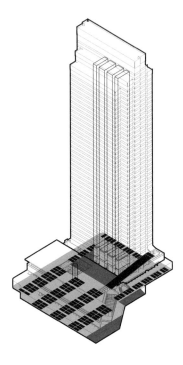

Embarcadero Center, San Francisco, CA

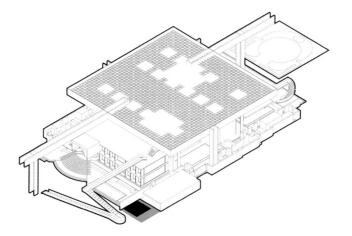

Entelechy II, Sea Island, GA

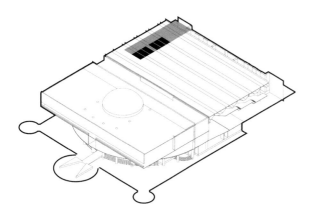

Emory University Student Center, Atlanta, GA

I don't know what the hell I'm going to do next, I really don't. But I know how I'm going to approach it; I know the way I am, the way I feel, the way I see.

JP

Nine Persuasions towards Architectural Pizzazz through the Work of John Portman

Jennifer Bonner

1. Architectural pizzazz is overturning assumptions about the ordinary.

Familiar or conventional spaces such as a basement ought not to be labelled "basement" in the work of John Portman. The dark ancillary leftover space of a building is reconceived as a sunken atrium for displaying art. At the SunTrust Plaza tower in Atlanta, paintings, sculptures, and furniture created by the architect, along with works by other artists, are on view in a top-lit subterranean space, accessible via a public sidewalk from Peachtree Street or through an elevated sky bridge. It cannot get more fabulous than this: an art gallery with a Jean Dubuffet and rare Portman furniture tucked away in a sunken atrium for all those who happen to stumble indoors.

2. Architectural pizzazz is amplifying the interior.

When an urban site was too small to accommodate the typical Portmanian strategy of hotel rooms encircling a superatrium, the architect adjusted his diagram. At the Westin Peachtree Plaza in Atlanta, the atrium was omitted and hotel rooms were wrapped around a circulation core in a cylindrical fashion. This allowed Portman to shift the focus of the design from the atrium to the spatiality of the 90-foot-tall hotel lobby. With a stretched ceiling height and large reflecting pools, Portman achieves a sparkly interior. The second instance of a sparkly effect can be found in the highly reflective glass facade of the cylindrical tower. (See note 5 below for more persuasions on the cylinder.) When the hotel opened its doors in 1976, guests lounged in cocktail pods that floated like islands in the lobby's artificial ponds. Ten years later, the pools were drained to make way for a series of architectural follies—colonnades and pediments in a pastel color palette. But version 2.0 of the lobby is far from normal. The classical pediment is stretched and elongated to fill out the ceiling of the vertical lobby, disobeying all classical proportions. With cocktail glasses in hand, guests turn their attention upwards—from the wet floor towards charming pavilions and dangling glass chandeliers. When making sizeable public spaces, Portman amplifies two primary interior surfaces: the ground and ceiling.

3. Architectural pizzazz is an architecture that rotates.

At the tip-top of the 73-story Westin Peachtree Plaza tower is a double-decker architectural turntable. A restaurant and a mezzanine lounge rotate around a shared core; a full revolution takes one hour and offers a 360-degree view of the city. The allure of this kind of space is that it is both disorientating and magical. Depending on the weather or the time of day, one can take in a sunset, ride in the clouds, or monitor an impending tornado. Another rotating space in Atlanta is the Polaris, a flying saucer–like restaurant perched atop Portman's Hyatt Regency. From inside this glowing blue dome, visitors can spy on the city below. They might observe increased construction activity at the new Falcon's stadium, or ponder Stone Mountain, that large rock located due east of the city. Several contemporary architects are working on the problem of kinetic architecture; others are using revolution as a technique for formal experimentation. Regardless of the direction rotation takes in contemporary architectural discourse, Portman continues to seductively spin space around and around. Rotating Portman architecture, which is also found in New York and Los Angeles, creates a top-floor urbanism. Vertigo-inducing and dizzying, architectural pizzazz provides glammed-up views of the city.

4. Architectural pizzazz is overstating the corner.

With a kind of exotic magnetism, four spiral staircases in Building 3 of Portman's AmericasMart in Atlanta substantiate architecture's corner problem. Portman designed the wholesale trade center in phases, entertaining two readings of the architectural corner over a nine-year period. In the 1979 version, the spiral stairs are tower-like figures detached from the building's mass that purposely define the corners from what otherwise reads, when viewed from the street, as a five-story blank facade. After an addition was completed in 1988, the spiral stairs read as columns holding up the additional floor plates. Regardless of the two latent readings of the project, these urban spiral staircases—intentionally scaled up from the familiar domestic ones—point our attention to the corner's form. Sure, architects have embraced fire stairs and vertical circulation as exterior appendages to buildings before. But the takeaway here is how the architect defines the corner one way, and then nine years later challenges his own interpretation. Architectural pizzazz is exuberant corners, not the boring minimal kind.

5. Architectural pizzazz is the faceted condition of the extruded cylinder type.

The extruded cylindrical towers of Detroit's Renaissance Center, Los Angeles's Westin Bonaventure, and Atlanta's Westin Peachtree Plaza can be traced to an architectural experiment tucked away in the backyard of Portman's first superatrium hotel. After it opened in 1967, the Hyatt Regency Atlanta maintained maximum occupancy. Portman was asked to build more rooms within the same development. He responded by designing a tower that not only provided more square footage but also served as a full-scale mockup to test his ideas on the cylinder type. Made of black steel and faceted smoky-gray glass, the Ivy Tower, completed in 1971, was at the time a new formal investigation for Portman's office. It is common practice for architects to require mock-ups prior to the start of construction in order to test material assembly and construction techniques with the contractor, but Portman used the mock-up to experiment with faceted radii. The cylindrical projects that followed the Ivy Tower are much taller and bulkier, making this initial experiment look like a miniature. As the radii of the cylinder increases, the treatment of the facet becomes important. Since facets are reflective, the original form is distorted even further. Facets provide spectral oomph; but in more straightforward terms they rationalize geometry. Currently in the architectural discipline, smoothness is being pursued with algorithms and Grasshopper sliders. However, the sparkly effect of the facet in Portman's cylinders demands a second look.

6. Architectural pizzazz is the use of glass elevators.

Portman deploys a combination of glass and closed-cabin elevators in several projects. The architect's first attempt at the designing the glass elevator coincided with the birth of the superatrium. The glass cabin is necessary to fully experience the 27-story void at the center of the Hyatt Regency Atlanta. Three capsule-like elevators (patented by Portman) proudly hum up and down the exposed elevator core like bedazzled jewels. At the Marriott Marquis in Atlanta, guests are thrust via glass elevators into the spectacular section of the atrium as floor plates and corridors fan away from the viewer. In other words, the guest is absorbed into the deep sectioning of the architecture and invited to participate in it. Whimsical and slightly unbelievable, this experience counters the Ferris-wheel-gimmick-as-urban-ride of Las Vegas's High Roller, Singapore's Flyer, or the London Eye. Whereas at these tourist

Overstating the Corner: Worm's-eye View of AmericasMart Building 3

Miniature Mock-up: Elevation Oblique of Ivy Tower

attractions thrill-seekers anticipate a ride from great heights, most hotel guests do not expect such a fantastical elevator ride (they were simply going to their hotel room). A few blocks from the Marquis, at the Westin Peachtree Plaza, the glass elevator is pushed from the center to the perimeter of the tower, allowing for a 73-level plummet into the city after drinks at the rotating Sundial restaurant. The circular plan of the tower is formally broken by the appendage, on the northeast side, of an elevator shaft. (From more southern parts of the city, the "bump" is hidden.) Architectural pizzazz never shuts off an interior experience, not even the momentary transition from floor to floor. Captivating interior architecture or urban views are constantly on display.

7. Architectural pizzazz is making additions on top of parking garages.

Portman's Courtland Street Parking Deck was built in 1985 to serve the Marquis Office Towers in downtown Atlanta. At first glance, the discreet concrete structure wrapped with vertical louvered slats seemed normal. But a triple-story break in the front facade suggested an alternate future for a structure whose sole purpose was to store the cars of employees of nearby office towers. Four years later, in keeping with the theme of renovation in Portman's projects, the Peachtree Center Athletic Club was added, boldly capping off the original parking structure with a mirrored glass form. The Athletic Club occupied the ninth and tenth floors of the parking garage, suggesting a penthouse condition to its members. A penthouse on top of a parking garage? It makes sense. As employees entered or left the parking garage each workday, they could pop up to the club for exercise. Most cities are filled with unsightly parking structures without architecture on top. Portman offers up a moment of architectural pizzazz in the most unexpected of places.

8. Architectural pizzazz is Tivoli lighting.

A single exposed light bulb seems commonplace, but when multiplied and arranged in a linear fashion, like in Portman's architecture, a grandiose lighting strategy is produced. Lining the underbelly of public spaces, exaggerating circulatory systems (escalators and elevator cabins), and encircling the top of a tower as a glowing ring, these lights underscore Portman's formal intentions. Tivoli lighting may accentuate a curve or direct movement in Portman's architecture, but ultimately it places emphasis on edges, figures, and shapes. These sparkly lights twinkle at the same time as they call attention to architectural volume.

9. Architectural pizzazz is reimagining the baroque.

Over the span of two decades, before expanding his architectural repertoire into something other, Portman designed numerous classical spaces composed largely of symmetrical primitive volumes. With the completion of the Marriott Marquis in Atlanta, in 1986, Portman's cubes and cylinders merged into a parabola for the first time. The 52-level parabolic tower marks a shift in posture. The concrete plasticity and tapering section (no two floor plates are the same) of the Marquis is not an advancement on the super-atrium, as most historians and contemporary architects suggest, but rather Portman's move to re-evaluate the baroque. While symmetry can still be spotted in the short section, asymmetry occurs in the long section (the atrium is subdivided by a bank of elevators, allowing for two pockets of supertall space to unfold). Portman's authoring of novel space is like the baroque architects of 17th-century Italy who were misbehaving with the classical proportions established by the Renaissance. Except, instead of referring to a shift in disciplinary paradigms, he's simply practicing with his own original forms. Step onto one of the many levels at the base of the Marriott Marquis tower, and visitors will find a glamorous view of Portman's baroque.

Architectural pizzazz, with all its flair, zest, and sparkle, is rarely discussed within the discipline of architecture. "Pizzazz," a term coined by a *Harper's Bazaar* fashion editor in 1937, is most closely associated with style, which is frowned upon in architectural discourse. This essay argues for new terminology and offers ways of extracting ideologies from a Southern architecture that has been largely overlooked in our field. The work of Atlanta-based architect John Portman invites contemporary architects to rethink the essence of their individual projects in terms of architectural pizzazz. The nine persuasions outlined here collapse architectural details with form in an attempt to merge affect with typology.

If the debate between "less is more" and "less is a bore" is still alive (and the stark differences among camps in contemporary architecture tell us it is), then architectural pizzazz is more closely aligned with the latter, since Portman's architecture radiates with charm, oomph, and allure.

Image Credits

10: Andreas Gursky, *Atlanta,* 1996, C-Print, 180 × 253 × 6.2 cm. © Andreas Gursky / 2017, ProLitteris, Zürich. Courtesy: Sprüth Magers Berlin London.

12: © Jordi Bernadó. Courtesy Ramon Prat.

38: John Portman and Associates, The Entelechy I Collection, The Portman Archives, LLC.

54, 55 middle, bottom: John Portman and Associates, The Entelechy II Collection, The Portman Archives, LLC.

55 top: Helmut Jacoby, The Entelechy II Collection, The Portman Archives, LLC.

84: John C. Portman and Associates, The Atlanta Apparel Mart Collection, The Portman Archives, LLC.

108: Edwards and Portman, The Peachtree Center Collection, The Portman Archives, LLC.

109 top right: J. Jones, The Peachtree Center Collection, The Portman Archives, LLC.

109 second from bottom: The Peachtree Center Collection, The Portman Archives, LLC.

109 top left, middle, bottom: John Portman and Associates, The Peachtree Center Collection, The Portman Archives, LLC.

128 top, 129 top left, bottom: John Portman and Associates, The Hyatt Regency Atlanta Collection, The Portman Archives, LLC.

128 bottom: Edwards and Portman, The Hyatt Regency Atlanta Collection, The Portman Archives, LLC.

129 top right: J.N. Smith, The Hyatt Regency Atlanta Collection, The Portman Archives, LLC.

140 top: Phillip Vullo, The Westin Peachtree Plaza Collection, The Portman Archives, LLC.

140 bottom left: John C. Portman, Jr., The Westin Peachtree Plaza Collection, The Portman Archives, LLC.

140 bottom right, 137: John Portman and Associates, The Westin Peachtree Plaza Collection, The Portman Archives, LLC.

150–151: John Portman and Associates, The Atlanta Marriott Marquis Collection, The Portman Archives, LLC.

190: John Portman and Associates, The Emory University Student Center Collection, The Portman Archives, LLC.

196 top, middle: Dan Harmon, The Renaissance Center Collection, The Portman Archives, LLC.

196 bottom: Unknown renderer, Renaissance Center Collection, The Portman Archives, LLC.

197: John Portman and Associates, The Renaissance Center Collection, The Portman Archives, LLC.

212 left: John Portman and Associates, The Embarcadero Center West Collection, The Portman Archives, LLC.

212 right, 220: John Portman and Associates, The Embarcadero Center Collection, The Portman Archives, LLC.

230: John Portman and Associates, The New York Marriott Marquis Collection, The Portman Archives, LLC.

242 top left: Richard Gardner, The Westin Peachtree Plaza Collection, The Portman Archives, LLC.

242 top right, bottom, 239: John Portman and Associates, The Westin Bonaventure Collection, The Portman Archives, LLC.

260, 266 bottom, 267 top: © Charles Rice.

263 top: Scottish National Gallery.

263 bottom, 266 top: Amit Geron, © PSC, Inc.

267 bottom: Michael Portman, The Portman Archives, LLC.

346–347: Jennifer Bonner and Stephanie Conlan. Courtesy of MALL.

Photography by Iwan Baan:
39–53, 57–73, 75–83, 85–97, 98–107, 110–127, 130–139, 142–149, 152–169, 171–181, 183–189, 191–195, 199–211, 214–219, 221–229, 231–241, 244–259, 276–277

Contributors' Biographies

Iwan Baan

Dutch photographer Iwan Baan is known primarily for images that narrate the life and interactions that occur within architecture. Baan's photographs reveal our innate ability to reappropriate our available objects and materials in order to find a place we can call our own. Architects such as Rem Koolhaas, Herzog & de Meuron, Zaha Hadid, SANAA, and Morphosis turn to Baan to give their work a sense of place and narrative within their environments. Alongside his architecture commissions, Baan has collaborated on several book projects such as *Insular Insight: Where Art and Architecture Conspire with Nature* (2011), *Torre David: Informal Vertical Communities* (2012), and *Brasilia–Chandigarh: Living with Modernity* (2010). He was the inaugural recipient of the Julius Shulman Institute Excellence in Photography Award.

Jennifer Bonner

Jennifer Bonner is assistant professor at the Harvard University Graduate School of Design and director of MALL. Born in Alabama, Jennifer received a bachelor of architecture from Auburn University and a master of architecture from Harvard University. She is founder of A Guide to the Dirty South, a book series with forthcoming titles on Atlanta and New Orleans, guest editor of *ART PAPERS* Special Architecture and Design Issue on Los Angeles, and editor of Harvard GSD's *Platform: Still Life*. Bonner has exhibited her work at numerous institutions including the Istanbul Design Biennial and HistoryMIAMI.

Preston Scott Cohen

Preston Scott Cohen is the Gerald M. McCue Professor of Architecture at the Harvard University Graduate School of Design and principal of Preston Scott Cohen, Inc., a firm based in Cambridge, Massachusetts. He is the author of *Contested Symmetries* (2001) and numerous theoretical and historical essays on architecture. His work has been widely exhibited and is in numerous collections, including the Museum of Modern Art, New York; Cooper Hewitt, Smithsonian Design Museum; San Francisco Museum of Modern Art; Museum of Contemporary Art, Los Angeles; and Fogg Museum, Harvard University.

Merrill Elam

Merrill Elam is a principal of Mack Scogin Merrill Elam Architects, a firm based in Atlanta, Georgia. She lectures and teaches frequently, and has served as visiting professor at the Georgia Institute of Technology, visiting professor at the Southern California Institute of Architecture, the Harry S. Shure Visiting Professor in Architecture at the University of Virginia, and visiting critic at the Harvard Graduate School of Design. With Mack Scogin, she received the 2012 Cooper Hewitt National Design Award for Architecture and the 2011 Arnold W. Brunner Memorial Prize from the American Academy of Arts and Letters. Elam holds a bachelor of architecture from the Georgia Institute of Technology and a master of business administration from Georgia State University.

K. Michael Hays

K. Michael Hays is the Eliot Noyes Professor of Architectural Theory and associate dean for academic affairs at the Harvard University Graduate School of Design, where he also serves as interim chair of the Department of Architecture. His research and scholarship have focused on the areas of European modernism and critical theory, as well as on theoretical issues in contemporary architectural practice. He has published on the work of modern architects such as Hannes Meyer, Ludwig Hilberseimer, and Mies van der Rohe, in addition to contemporary figures such as Peter Eisenman, Bernard Tschumi, and John Hejduk. Hays was the founder of the scholarly journal *Assemblage*, which was a leading forum of discussion of architectural theory in North America and Europe.

Mohsen Mostafavi

Mohsen Mostafavi, architect and educator, is the Dean of the Harvard Graduate School of Design and the Alexander and Victoria Wiley Professor of Design. His work focuses on modes and processes of urbanization and on the interface between technology and aesthetics. Previously, he was the chairman of the Architectural Association School of Architecture in London. His books include *On Weathering: The Life of Buildings in Time* (coauthored 1993), which received the American Institute of Architects prize for writing on architectural theory; *Ecological Urbanism* (coedited 2010); *Nicholas Hawksmoor: London Churches* (2015); and *Ethics of the Urban: The City and the Spaces of the Political* (2017).

Alexander S. Porter

Alexander S. Porter is a masters of architecture student at Harvard University. He will graduate in the spring of 2018, after which he hopes to pursue his research interests through continued academic and professional engagements, as well as writing. Alexander holds a bachelor's degree from Columbia University in music and architecture, earning departmental honors for his thesis.

Mack Scogin

Mack Scogin is a principal of Mack Scogin Merrill Elam Architects, a firm based in Atlanta, Georgia. He is the Kajima Professor in Practice of Architecture at the Harvard University Graduate School of Design, where he was the chairman of the Department of Architecture from 1990 to 1995. With Merrill Elam, he received the 1995 Academy Award in Architecture from the American Academy of Arts and Letters; a 1996 Chrysler Award for Innovation in Design; the 2006 Boston Society of Architects Harleston Parker Medal; and a 2008 Honorary Fellowship in the Royal Institute of British Architects (RIBA). Projects by Mack Scogin Merrill Elam Architects have received over fifty design awards, including six national American Institute of Architects Awards of Excellence.

Mickey Steinberg

Mickey Steinberg is senior advisor to the executive leadership at Portman Holdings. He previously served as executive vice president of the Portman Companies for 20 years, with responsibilities in the operations of the architecture, development, management, and finance components of the organization. Since leaving Portman Holdings, Steinberg has served as executive vice president and chief operating officer of Walt Disney Imagineering, as well as chairman and chief executive officer of Sony Retail Entertainment. Steinberg holds a bachelor of science and a bachelor of architecture from the Georgia Institute of Technology, and a master of architecture from the Massachusetts Institute of Technology.